THE SCIENCE OF ANIMAL WELFARE

Animal Suffering

THE SCIENCE OF ANIMAL WELFARE

Marian Stamp Dawkins

M.A., D.Phil.

Mary Snow Fellow in Biological Sciences
Somerville College, Oxford

LONDON   NEW YORK
CHAPMAN AND HALL

First published 1980 by
Chapman and Hall Ltd,
11 New Fetter Lane, London EC4P 4EE
Reprinted 1988

Published in the USA by
Chapman and Hall
29 West 35th Street, New York, NY 10001

© 1980 Marian Stamp Dawkins

Printed in Great Britain by
J. W. Arrowsmith Ltd,
Bristol

ISBN 0 412 22580 8 (hardback)
ISBN 0 412 22590 5 (paperback)

British Library Cataloguing in Publication Data

Dawkins, Marian
  Animal suffering.
  1. Animals, Treatment of
  I. Title
  179'.3   HV4708   80–49954

  ISBN 0–412–22580–8
  ISBN 0–412–22590–5 Pbk

Contents

Preface

I wrote this book because I believe that the welfare of animals is a very important subject but one about which there is a great deal of confusion and muddled thinking. I wanted to write a book which straightened out some of the confusion by looking in detail at one particular problem: how to recognize animal suffering.

The book is written for anyone interested in animals and the controversies over how human beings should treat them. I have tried to convince people who might otherwise feel that science had only a rather sinister connection with animal welfare that the scientific study of animal suffering has, in fact, a major and positive contribution to make. It can give us an insight into what animals experience and this, in turn, may help us to alleviate their suffering.

At the same time, I have tried to write a book that will be of at least some use to scientists. The chapters which follow provide an outline of the biological approach to animal welfare. I have also attempted to show sceptics that it is possible to study animal suffering without sacrificing standards of scientific procedure. Perhaps some may even come to share my belief that the study of the subjective experiences of animals is one of the most fascinating areas in the whole of biology, as well as being of great practical and ethical importance.

Writing a book for both non-biologists and biologists is not easy. The compromise I have adopted is to write in a way which does not assume any specialist knowledge, but to provide full references at the end for those who wish to pursue individual topics more fully.

I am aware that I may be accused of sitting on a fence. It is true that I have tended to describe and analyse controversies rather than to come out firmly on one side or the other. But this is deliberate. There are so many strongly held views about animal welfare that I felt it was more constructive in the long run to give an account of a field of study than to air my own opinions, although these will inevitably show through in places. I should say, however, that a conviction that our treatment of animals is not all it should be was one of my main motives for writing a book in the first place.

I would like to thank Lesley Brown, Richard Dawkins, David Macdonald and Roger Tarpy for their comments on various chapters. Robert Drewett kindly read the whole manuscript and made some important criticisms.

I am particularly grateful to Colin Clark for valuable suggestions and guidance in that most difficult aspect, the style and 'tone' of the writing.

1   *Introduction*

None of us can escape contact with animals. Our food, clothing and medicines depend on animals. Pest animals are killed because they eat our food or interfere with our lives. Animals are companions, guides and quarry for sport.

More and more people are becoming concerned that animals suffer from their contact with us. Farming, particularly some intensive methods of keeping calves, chickens and pigs, has come in for a great deal of criticism. So has the culling of seals and the use of animals in research and medicine. The arguments which take place about these issues are often bitter and passionate, with accusations of 'torture' or 'concentration camp methods' against farmers and scientists.

There are many reasons why the treatment of animals arouses such controversy, but one of the main ones is a failure to agree on how to recognize and define 'suffering'. Some people, for example, claim that farm animals cannot possibly be suffering in intensive systems because they are so productive. Other people will claim, with just as much conviction, that they certainly *do* suffer because they are so restricted. Each side is using a different method for assessing the welfare of the animals and coming up with a completely different answer. Deciding which method or methods give the most reliable indications of animal suffering could therefore make a crucial contribution to debates about animal welfare.

This book is about such methods. It is an attempt to evaluate the various ways which have been proposed for

1

assessing suffering in animals, particularly suffering that may occur when there are no obvious signs of physical ill-health or injury. It is emphatically not a campaign for or against any particular way of treating animals. Nor is it an account of the conditions in which animals are kept or the things that are done to them. The only thing it sets out to do is to provide a basis for answering the question: 'How do we *know* this animal is suffering?', when that animal may be in a zoo, a farm, a laboratory, or anywhere else.

There may be some people who feel that it is quite unnecessary to go into methods in such details ("I don't need a book to tell me what's cruel to animals"). But, as will become more obvious later, we do not know infallibly what the mental experiences of other animals are like, particularly those of animals that are structurally very different from us. And, if people feel that it is important to try to change the laws about the treatment of animals, they must have more to go on than just their intuition. 'Suffering' must be recognizable in some objective way. Otherwise the laws which emerge are almost bound to be arbitrary and might even fail to improve the lot of the animals much, if at all.

There may be other people, particularly scientists, who feel that it is quite impossible to study animal suffering in an objective scientific way because of the subjective overtones. The difficulties of studying the subjective experiences of animals are certainly much greater than those of studying something which can be measured directly, such as the length of their bones. As we shall see in Chapter 2, however, growing numbers of scientists are now studying the mental experiences of animals in a rigorous and experimental way.

The argument throughout this book will be that there is no single method which, by itself, can tell us about the emotional experiences that animals might have. In Chapters 3 to 8, we will see that each of the ways that have so far been used – physiology, behaviour, productivity and so on – have their own particular shortcomings. Each one is inadequate if used on its own. What is necessary is a synthesis of the pictures given by all methods, as discussed in Chapter 9. We have to look, as it were, through many windows into a room that may look slightly different through each one. Otherwise we are like the blind men all feeling an elephant. Grabbing the tail and claiming that an elephant is a rope or holding a leg and claiming that an elephant is a tree trunk is very similar to basing arguments about animal welfare on only one sort of information.

Methods for assessing suffering are not, of course, the only reason that people disagree about the treatment of animals. In this chapter we will begin by looking at some of the other major causes of controversy. Then, we will look at the various ways in which people have regarded the two issues of killing animals and inflicting suffering on them while they are alive. Finally, we will touch upon some of the anomalies that beset discussions about animal welfare, a theme we will return to at the end of the book. This introduction thus sets the stage for the subsequent chapters on methods for assessing animal suffering.

Some sources of disagreement

Even people with basically similar views about animals can get very angry with each other because they disagree about what actually takes place. For example, a great deal of controversy has arisen over whether most experiments on animals are done for medical purposes or not. All experiments in Britain which are calculated to cause pain or suffering must be licensed by the Home Office, and Ryder [169] claimed that two-thirds of these are done for the purpose of testing non-medical products such as cosmetics and toiletries.

Shuster [181], however, insisted that only $1-2\%$ of animal experiments were to do with cosmetics. He reckoned that 75% of all licensed experiments are concerned with medical research and drug testing, with many of the rest being related to medical problems, such as tissue transplantation. The difference of opinion came from the interpretation of the two-thirds of all licensed experiments the purpose of which was not described by the Home Office in their report for 1975. One third of licensed experiments were said to be for cancer research, diagnosis and the legally required testing of drugs. Ryder had interpreted this to mean that all the rest were non-medical. But Shuster pointed out that it was not clear what they were for because the Home Office had not provided details of their purpose. The Home Office Report for 1977 [86] suggested that the mystery two-thirds were, in fact, mostly to do with the selection of new drugs, and the 1978 Report [87], which supplied much more information, states that over half the experiments (56%) were "performed to select, develop or study the use, hazards or safety of medical, dental or veterinary products or appliances". Over one-fifth (22%) were performed to study body structure or function and a further fifth to fulfill legal requirements for the testing of non-medical products such as food additives, herbicides and cosmetics. But less than 1% of the total number of licensed experiments performed in 1978 were to do with cosmetics and toiletries.

These figures are not being used to argue one way or the other on the question of whether these experiments were justified. The point of quoting them is simply to illustrate how arguments which appear on the surface to be dis-agreements about moral beliefs may turn out to be essentially factual in origin. People do, of course, genuinely differ in the way they think animal suffering should be weighed against possible value to human health, but they may have basically similar views on this matter and yet still disagree fiercely about animal experiments, because some start with the premise that most are medical and others assume that most are not.

The word 'experiment' itself, incidentally, is a good example of the confusion that can exist in peoples' minds because of basic misunderstandings about facts. The only thing which distinguishes an experiment from any other procedure is that the result should not be known beforehand (e.g. Littlewood Report [128]). Giving a pigeon a choice between maize and peas, for example, could constitute an experiment on food preference. The experiment might consist of nothing more than allowing the bird to walk between different food dishes and eat what it liked. On the other hand, using an animal to culture viruses within its living body, to produce antibodies to a disease, or as a source of tissue, do not, technically, count as experiments because these are routine procedures for which the outcome is known. To make vaccines (which do not count as experiments), animals may be deliberately infected with debilitating diseases. The Littlewood Committee argued that such treatments may cause more suffering than would be allowed by law in any experiment.

In other words, an experiment does not cause suffering just because it is an experiment. Nor are non-experimental procedures innocuous just because there is no experimental element.

Yet another source of friction is disagreement over the consequences of changing the way animals are treated. Two people could be totally opposed about how to treat farm animals or whether to allow certain sorts of tests on animals, purely on the basis of how acceptable they found alternative courses of action. One might believe, for instance, that it was quite unnecessary to test drugs on animals and would be quite prepared to give them to sick people without having tested them on other species first. The other might believe that this was much too high a price to pay. He might decide, reluctantly, that animal tests were necessary because he could not accept the consequences of doing without them.

The argument could become even more complicated if these two people also disagreed about whether adequate alternatives really existed to using living animals to test the safety of drugs, an issue discussed in detail by Smyth [188]. For example, the one who disagreed with animal experiments might believe that tissue culture methods could be used instead, whereas the other might be more sceptical and believe that tissue culture was a very unreliable way of screening substances for human consumption. Here too, the disagreement need not necessarily be over moral values. It could arise purely from different interpretations or amounts of knowledge about facts, in this case, facts about tissue culture.

A double standard: suffering and death

Another reason for controversy is the different attitudes that people can take up over the two issues of killing animals and causing them to suffer when they are alive. It is a striking fact that many animal welfare organizations kill large numbers of animals. The Littlewood Report [128] estimates that in 1963, for example, the RSPCA killed over 20 000 unwanted dogs and cats, more than the number used in licensed experiments in Britain that year. And the World Federation for the Protection of Animals estimates that, throughout Europe, some 5 million dogs are destroyed each year because they are unwanted, many by animal welfare organizations [23].

A great many people who are very concerned about the welfare of animals also eat the dead bodies of those same animals. 'Factory farming' methods and the shipment of live cattle disturb them not because the animals will eventually be killed and eaten, but more because of the possible suffering they experience when they are alive. They do not necessarily object to the slaughter of animals, but they do want it to be 'humane'.

Most of the people who hold such views about animals, however, would be quite horrified at the idea of the 'humane slaughter' of old or sick humans. 'Putting down' unwanted children or cultivating people, even in luxurious surroundings for the purpose of killing them and eating them later, would be quite unthinkable. There is, therefore, a very widespread double standard even amongst people who are very concerned about animal welfare. Killing human beings is regarded as wrong, even to put them out of their misery. Eating people is even worse. But killing animals for food is usually regarded as preferable to keeping them alive and in pain.

A few people reject this double standard. Godlovitch [69] argues that it does not make sense to say that you care about the suffering of animals and then to say that you do not care whether they are alive or dead. She believes that caring about an animal cannot involve killing and eating it. Brophy [19] makes a similar point: "I do not for a moment admit your right to kill me provided you do it by creeping up on me and contriving not to give me pain and fear"; Harris [75] writes uncompromisingly: "To continue to eat the object of your concern is a stunning piece of self-deception".

'Animal welfare', therefore, means very different things to different people. To some people it means the physical and mental well-being of animals while they are alive. They may want to eat pigs, but they want to be sure that the pigs they eat have lived lives free of suffering. But to other people, concern for the welfare of an animal cannot involve killing it. They see being eaten as an insurmountable obstacle to any pig's welfare.

This fundamental difference in attitudes to killing animals means that people concerned with 'animal welfare' may, in fact, have very different aims. Some are opposed to the whole idea of 'exploiting' animals. They feel it is wrong to eat animals or to exert any sort of control over pest animals, for instance. Other peoples' aims will be much more restricted. They will accept killing animals for food, but will be opposed to keeping them under intensive indoor systems of management. Or, they may accept the need for killing pest animals, but will be concerned to find humane ways of doing this. Yet other people, also wanting to reduce animal suffering, will have even more modest goals. They will not only believe that it is necessary to kill animals, they may also believe that practices such as intensive farming are essential too. Their main aim will be to see that, within the intensive farm, the animals' welfare is as good as possible. They may be concerned, for example, to increase the space allowed to each chicken or each pig within its cage. But this would be considered as mere tinkering with details by someone with more radical views whose aim was to abolish intensive farming altogether.

Thus, even ardent campaigners for animal welfare differ in what they are actually trying to achieve. A fundamental reason for this is a split over the issues of suffering and death and of whether the same standards should apply to other species as they do to human beings.

More anomalies: appealing species and rare species

Some animals undoubtedly have an advantage over others when it comes to arousing human sympathy. Dogs, cats and horses receive special protection under British law, which reflects peoples' attitudes to them as companions and friends. The idea of eating dog steak or horse stew is abhorrent even to many non-vegetarians.

Other kinds of animals appeal to human emotions because of what they look like. Helpless baby seals with large brown eyes and rounded faces have a great advantage in this respect over adult rats with yellow teeth and long pink tails. A large colour poster of a baby seal makes it very easy to forget that seals are regarded as a serious pest by many fishermen. A large colour poster of a rat is unlikely to arouse the same sort of sympathy. People do not get upset about poisoning rats even though poisons may cause severe convulsions before death. People simply do not like rats and are consequently much less concerned about their welfare than that of, say, their pet kittens.

There is also a widespread feeling that is more important to be concerned about the welfare of endangered species, such as whales or tigers, than that of commoner species such as foxes. Of course, there are many good reasons for wanting to prevent species from becoming extinct. But as far as the individual animal is concerned, it can suffer just as much if it is one of many millions as if it were the last survivor. Suffering is an individual matter, not a property of a species. The fact that there are 'plenty more where that came from' does not lessen an individual animal's experience of pain or suffering.

There are thus many anomalies in the way that people care for animals. From the list of species that generates the most concern, it would sometimes seem that suffering was only experienced by the rare and the beautiful or by animals that happen to look noble like stags and eagles. Human whim and fancy play a major part in deciding which species are cared for and which are not.

Assessment of suffering and debates about animal welfare

To have plunged straight into a discussion of the methods which might be used to assess animal suffering without mentioning any of the other problems would have been very misleading. It would have suggested that all that was needed was a bit of calm discussion about such methods and the controversies would disappear. But as we have seen, there are disagreements at every step of the way, even amongst people who are concerned that animals should not suffer.

Collecting basic factual information about what happens to animals in zoos, farms, laboratories, petshops and other places where they are kept is of great importance in resolving at least some of these disagreements. It is at least a first step. The second is to decide whether those animals are suffering or not, by using some or all of the criteria discussed in the following chapters. Even then we are not out of the wood. We still have to face the political, social and economic consequences of any decisions about, say, altering the law on the treatment of animals. We may have to decide priorities, perhaps between human welfare and that of other species. These are very important issues, but separate from the main concern of this book: the assessment of suffering itself.

Looking closely at the ways in which this might be done is an attempt to clarify one area of confusion. It is not a hair-splitting exercise and certainly not an attempt to cover up genuine suffering where it occurs. The book is written out of respect for animals and a concern for their welfare. It is also written in protest against the view that it is unnecessary to make any effort to understand what animal suffering might be like. As Medawar [139] wrote: "The welfare of animals must depend on an *understanding* of animals, and one does not come by this understanding intuitively: it must be learned".

2   *The subjective experience of animals*

How can we study the welfare of animals? 'Welfare' means not just physical well-being and the absence of disease and injury; to most people it also means mental well-being. How can we find out whether an animal is in a state of mental well-being or whether it is suffering? For that matter, how can we find out about any of the subjective experiences that animals might have?

Before we can discuss the ways in which animal suffering might be assessed, we have to be sure that the mental experiences of animals can be studied at all. Many scientists believe that the subjective worlds of animals are not open to investigation. They see 'consciousness' and 'suffering' as unscientific concepts. In their eyes, there could not be a scientific study of animal suffering. It would be a contradiction in terms. This chapter will attempt to show that the subjective experiences of animals can be studied, and studied scientifically. In the first section, we will discuss the very great difficulties of studying any subjective phenomena in animals. But in the second section we will see that these difficulties may not be as great as they sometimes seem. During the last few years, there has been something of a revolution in the attitudes of some scientists towards the study of mental events. We will see that this has important implications for animal welfare.

It is first necessary to make a disclaimer for this chapter. It will not attempt to be concerned with the complex philosophical problems about the relationship between mind and body. These problems, such as whether 'mind' and 'body' are two separate entities, remain as baffling as ever and they are completely outside the scope of this book. The apparent revolution in the attitude of some scientists has not come from solving any deep philosophical problems, but from simply accepting that some bodily states and behaviour can be used as reasonably reliable guides to what a human or other animal is experiencing. This may seem obvious to someone unfamiliar with the scientific way of looking at things. What, they might feel, is all the fuss about? Why is it so difficult to study mental experiences in animals? Why could we not get straight on with the task of assessing animal welfare, mental as well as physical? Let us see why.

The scientific objections

Subjective experiences, such as feelings of pleasure and pain, are difficult to study because of one unavoidable property: they are essentially private. We may each experience vivid feelings of pain or thirst or happiness, but each individual can experience only his own feelings. Other people can see the external signs, such as facial expressions. They may even be able to measure physiological changes, such as heart-rate. But as Skinner [186] put it, where our feelings are concerned, we are locked within our own skins.

Because nobody can have access to what another person is experiencing, the normal methods of science, which involve independent testing of hypotheses by different observers, simply do not work. There is only ever one observer and his observations cannot be checked. Many behavioural scientists have therefore taken the view that no mental phenomena can be studied scientifically. One of the most influential of these was Watson [205] who wrote in no uncertain terms over sixty years ago: "'States of consciousness' like the so-called phenomena of spiritualism are not objectively verifiable and for that reason can never become data for science". Watson believed that science should only be concerned with what animals and people do, not with what they experience. A great many scientists since have agreed with him. They are known as 'Behaviourists' to emphasize that they study behaviour (and physiology), but not mental events.

It is perhaps important to distinguish two varieties of Behaviourism, although in practice the borderline between them is often indistinct. There is what has been called 'methodological Behaviourism' which is the attitude that although subjective experiences may exist, it is no concern of science to study them. Subjective experiences are thus simply ignored. Then there is also 'logical Behaviourism', which is the view that any statements about mental events are actually meaningless. Here, subjective experiences are not merely ignored, they are defined out of existence. So, to a Logical Behaviourist, to desire food is seen as nothing more than to engage in eating, to feel pain is to writhe, groan and so on. There is nothing 'extra' which could be described as feeling hungry or being in pain, since the only real phenomena are held to be behavioural and physiological ones.

As Griffin [70] has pointed out, there have been some unfortunate results of confusing these two sorts of Behaviourism. Many scientists may have originally adopted the Behaviourist attitude to mental events as a way of making their science rigorous. But having done this, they began to see mental events as not merely awkward to deal with, but having no reality. Banished from science for methodological reasons, mental events, particularly those in non-human species, were then denied an existence altogether.

Klopfer and Hailman [115] and Griffin [70] stress the enormous impact which Behaviourism, of both sorts, has had on scientific research in this century. They argue that it has prevented most scientists from making any reference to the subjective experiences their animals might have. Workers may secretly have believed that 'something was missing' from their accounts of animal behaviour because they did not do so. But in public, and in print, they were Behaviourists.

All this might make Behaviourism an entirely negative philosophy. But even its critics, such as Hediger [77], who feel that it has been taken too far, admit that it has made a very positive contribution, too. It has helped people to think clearly, to formulate hypotheses which can be tested and not to see animals as little human beings in furry skins. Klopfer and Hailman [115] claim that in the nineteenth century, before Behaviourism was invented, there was no real science of animal behaviour at all, simply a collection of anecdotes. Behaviourism has helped to make animal behaviour into a scientific study, by forcing scientists to concentrate on what they can see and measure directly. Even then, they have run into difficulties, because animal behaviour is such a transient and variable phenomenon. But the difficulties would have been much greater if, at the same time, they had been trying to deal with postulated and unverifiable mental events.

In one important sense, Behaviourism is right. We cannot know for certain what an animal is experiencing, at least not in the way that we can see that it is eating or drinking. But does this mean that we should give up altogether and abandon all hope of learning anything at all about the subjective experiences of animals? In the next section, we will see that it does not.

Studying subjective experiences

One of the most unsatisfactory features of Behaviourism is the way it dismisses subjective experiences in other people. Strictly speaking, it says, you can never know that anyone has mental experiences except yourself. Most people, however, are quite content to believe that other people have feelings of suffering, pleasure and pain that are much like their own. Other peoples' behaviour and physiology are sufficiently like their own that this can be accepted without demanding logical proof.

The Behaviourists' insistence that we can never demonstrate subjective experiences in other people does not, therefore, carry much weight in everyday life. We do not see other people just as machines that produce grimaces and utterances, but we use these external signs as indications of what they are subjectively experiencing. The argument that we can never know that they are experiencing anything may be logical, but it is not very persuasive in practice.

Experimental psychologists have recently taken this commonsense view into the laboratory. They have assumed that people do have mental experiences and then devised experiments to investigate their nature and function, in direct defiance of Behaviourism. Sheehan [179] and Shepard [180], for example, have studied people's mental imagery experimentally. In a typical experiment, people would be asked to imagine a situation they cannot yet see and then tested for how quickly they react when they do see it. Being told to think about something in advance often helps people to react more quickly or to make more accurate discriminations (conversely, being told to think about the wrong thing holds them up). Of course, it does not follow that just because someone is told to imagine a situation and then deals with a similar real situation particularly well, that he has necessarily had a mental image of it. The strict Behaviourist could still object that this is a private experience which nobody else could know about for the reasons we have already discussed. But, though logical, this view no longer prevents the scientific investigation of mental images.

Among those who study non-human animals, there is also a growing interest in a wide variety of mental events and with it, a feeling that the Behaviouristic position is inadequate. This may look superficially as though people are reverting to a pre-Behaviouristic nineteenth-century view of animals, when Darwin [35], Romanes [164] and others had no qualms about discussing such states as jealousy, anger and sympathy in all sorts of animals including insects. This would, however, be misleading. Present day studies on the mental experiences of animals are far more rigorous and experimental than they were in the nineteenth century. The lessons of Behaviourism have not been lost. Perhaps the study of mental events in animals has advanced precisely because it has had to stand up to Behaviourists and justify itself in the face of their criticisms.

We will now look at some of the studies which have

explored the mental experiences of animals. We will be concerned not merely with *what* has been discovered, but *how* it has been discovered, as the claim that there can be a science of mental events in animals stands or falls by whether it is possible to devise tests of hypotheses and, if necessary, to discard them. If this is not possible, the Behaviourist would probably be quite justified in banishing mental events from scientific study.

We will begin historically, because it would be a mistake to leave the impression that all scientists in this century have been Behaviourists. Tolman, Yerkes and Köhler, amongst others, many years ago pioneered the experimental study of the mental life of animals. While the First World War raged in Europe, for example, Köhler [117] was sitting quietly on the island of Tenerife watching a group of captive chimpanzees. In his book *The Mentality of Apes*, Köhler describes his observations on the ability of the chimpanzees to obtain food that was out of their reach. He observed them piling boxes on top of one another to get at bananas suspended from the ceiling. He saw them skillfully use sticks to draw in objects that were more than an arm's length away from their cage, and if he did not give them ready made sticks, the chimpanzees would make their own by breaking off branches or gnawing wood into the right shape.

Köhler was particularly impressed by the suddenness with which the apes often appeared to find the solution to a problem he had set them. On one famous occasion, a male chimpanzee called Sultan tried in vain to reach some food which was lying just outside his cage. He was using a bamboo stick which was not long enough. Sultan had given up and was playing with two sticks in another part of his cage. He happened to fit one stick into the end of the other, making one long stick. Köhler argued that because Sultan immediately rushed back to the food, which was now well within the reach of his double stick, he must have 'realized' the importance of his accidental discovery.

Köhler also tested his chimpanzees on various complicated problems involving pulling strings or ropes. He modestly compared their impressive ability to know which string to select with his own inability to work out how to open up a folding deck chair. A recent observer of chimpanzees, Menzel [142], believes that, if anything, Köhler under-estimated what chimpanzees could do. For example, Köhler had seen chimpanzees apparently trying to make boxes stick to walls and concluded that they did not have a very good idea of how to build a stable structure. Menzel [143] describes how his chimpanzees built 'ladders' out of long poles and how they chose a position that was so stable that several chimpanzees at once could use it (and ruined his experiment because they kept getting out of their enclosure by climbing the ladders).

Köhler had also noticed that his apes were fascinated by their own reflections in a mirror or in a puddle of their urine. Recently, Gallup [64] has been able to show that chimpanzees probably realize that it is themselves they are looking at. Gallup [63] had previously shown that most species of animal respond to a mirror as if they were seeing another member of their own species. Male Siamese Fighting Fish, for example, threaten mirrors by raising their gill covers just as they do when they have seen another male fish. Very young human children, too, react to mirrors as if they were seeing someone else, at least until they are about 2 years old. Gallup argues that some retarded children seem incapable of ever recognizing their own reflections.

When Gallup first gave mirrors to a group of young, wild-born chimpanzees, they responded as if the animal in the mirror were another individual. But then, after 2 – 3 days, they began to use the mirror as if they were responding to themselves, for example, to groom parts of their bodies that they could not otherwise see.

The important point for our discussion is that Gallup did not stop at describing what he saw. He devised an experiment to test whether the chimpanzees really did regard their mirror reflections as being of themselves. His experiment involved giving the chimpanzees a light anaesthetic and then painting a non-irritant red dye on one of their eyebrows and the ear on the opposite side of the head. When they woke up from the anaesthetic, Gallup did not at first give them mirrors. He watched them carefully to see if they touched the dyed parts of their bodies, but they did not. When they were allowed to see themselves in a miror, however, they began repeatedly touching their own dyed ears and eyebrows, at the same time as intently examining their reflections. Other control chimpanzees which had been through the same treatment except that they had never had any previous experience with mirrors, did not touch their faces in this way. So it seems that experience with a mirror did result in a chimpanzee understanding what his reflection was.

The problem of whether it is possible to devise an experiment to show that animals are aware of what they are doing has been tackled by Beninger and his co-workers [12] with a particularly ingenious technique. They trained rats to press one of four levers depending on which of four behaviour patterns they were doing at the time when a buzzer sounded. For example, if the rat were washing its face when it heard the buzzer, it had to press one lever, which can be referred to as the face-washing lever, in order to get a piece of food. None of the other levers yielded food under these circumstances. Then, in another trial, the experimenters might press the buzzer when the rat was, say, rearing up on its hindlegs. Now the rat could only get food if it pressed the rearing lever and so on. The rats learnt to press a different lever depending on whether they were walking, rearing up, face-washing or remaining still.

Beninger *et al.* did not, however, immediately conclude that the rats were necessarily aware of which behaviour they were doing. They first tried to eliminate simpler hypotheses. For example, one possible explanation for their results was that the rats might just happen to do most of one behaviour in a particular place in the cage. So if the rat did most of its grooming in one corner, it might learn to make an association between that corner and getting food by pressing a particular lever. They therefore looked carefully to see whether the rats did have a tendency to behave in different ways in different parts of their cages and found that this could not explain the results. A team led by Morgan [147] repeated this experiment with similar results, although they were not quite as confident that they could rule out the 'particular place' explanation. Nevertheless, this technique is potentially a very powerful way of understanding what animals think they are doing, provided the right controls are done.

It is not only in mammals that scientists have been studying mental phenomena. Experiments on birds have produced some quite remarkable results. A pioneer in this field was Koehler [116] who demonstrated that birds are able to count or, as he put it, to "think unnamed numbers".

Koehler's experiments are worth describing in some detail because they illustrate how it is possible to eliminate alternatives to the hypothesis that animals really have the concept of number, by careful experimental design. One very likely alternative is that the animals do not really count at all, but respond to some subtle sign from the human beings watching them. Clever Hans was a horse who appeared to be able to do sums in his head and deliver the answer by striking his hoof on the ground the right number of times. It all looked very impressive until it was shown that the horse had learnt a relatively simple trick. He kept pawing the ground until he received a very small sign from his master that he had got to the right answer whereupon he stopped. The man was apparently unaware that he was doing anything at all.

To make certain that a similar effect did not operate with his birds, Koehler always watched the experiments from a separate room through a small camera viewfinder. The birds, which included a raven and a grey parrot, were trained to select one of a row of five small boxes, each of which had a different number (from $2-6$) of spots painted on the lid. The correct box (the only one containing food) was indicated on each trial by a 'sample' box placed in front of the test row. The bird had to look at the sample box, which might have anything from two to six spots on its lid, and then flip off the lid of the test box with the same number of spots. In order to make sure the bird did not just learn to open a box in a particular position, the positions of all the boxes were changed between each trial as was the number of spots on the sample box.

Koehler was also very concerned to make sure that the birds did not simply match one visual pattern with another. So he made the sample and test boxes look as different from one another as possible. The sample box might have a row of three small dots, for example, while the correct box to be chosen might have one small dot and two large splodges. One of the incorrect boxes might have four small dots and an overall appearance more like the sample than the correct box. The only thing which the sample and the correct test box had in common was the same number of 'somethings' on the lid. Only if the birds realized this could they solve the problem. Koehler's birds could correctly pick out 2, 3, 4, 5 or 6-spotted boxes even when the sample consisted of bits of broken plasticene without a box, so they seemed genuinely to have abstracted the concept of number.

Koehler's second test was even more ingenious. He trained the birds to take a certain number of pieces of food from the boxes and then stop. He hid the food in any one, or any combination, of seven small boxes. So, if the bird had been trained to take five bits of food, it might be able to find all five in the first box it opened or it might have to open anything up to seven. The number would vary from trial to trial. The only thing that remained constant was the number of bits of food the bird had to find before moving away from the boxes altogether. Koehler found that his birds could learn this task, flipping over lids until they had found the right number of baits and then, having done so, flying or walking away. They learnt not to go on looking once they had found the required number. Their concept of number in this case did not rest on how many boxes they had to open (because this varied from trial to trial), but on the remembered number of food items they were required to look for. One jackdaw became so good at this task that it could cope with several numbers at once, looking for different numbers of items depending on the colour of the boxes that Koehler laid out for it.

To claim that a bird can develop the concept of 'a human being' sounds, on the face of it, even more fanciful than the idea that it could count. But Herrnstein and Loveland [80] and Siegel and Honig [182] have been able to show experimentally that they do just that, and more. The way they did this was to present pigeons with many different coloured slides, some showing people, some animals, some buildings, some landscapes. They rewarded the pigeons with food if they pecked a certain key whenever any slide with a human being in it appeared, but not if they pecked when there was no human being in the picture. The slides with people in them were very variable. The showed children and adults, people of different races, people with clothes on and people without clothes, people sitting down or standing up, groups of people and people on their own and so on. So the pigeons could not simply learn to peck in the presence of a particular pattern of colour. They had to develop a generalized concept of a human being.

Herrnstein *et al.* [81] later showed that pigeons could learn to peck a key whenever they saw a picture of a particular person, whatever position she was in, but not when they saw a picture of anyone else. They could also be trained to recognize 'water'. They would peck one key whenever they saw any slide which had any water in it, whether it was a puddle on a muddy road or an aerial view of the Atlantic Ocean. But they would not peck this key if there was a picture with no water in it, even if the picture was otherwise similar, such as the road with no puddles. They could also recognize a 'tree' in the same way, when presented with pictures of many different sorts and sizes of trees. And they were not confused by objects which looked superficially like trees, such as a branching head of celery, which they did not classify as a 'tree'. The mistakes they made were most interesting. One slide was a picture of some houses with a tiny tree in the distance. Many human beings, when asked whether there was a tree in the picture said they could not see one until it was pointed out to them. The pigeons, too, tended to peck the key which signified 'no tree'.

An important features of these experiments is the way in which they were designed. Literally thousands of slides were presented to the pigeons to make sure they did not learn to respond to particular slides, and great care was taken over the choice of slides. Thus, some of the slides showed objects which were visually similar to each other but the pigeons had to classify them as different (such as celery and trees). But other slides were visually very different and the pigeons had to classify them as examples of the same concept (such as the different pictures of 'water'). Only by having both sorts of slides could it be concluded that the pigeons had developed a generalized and abstract concept that was not tied to details of the physical appearance of particular objects.

If experiments are not well designed, it is easy to believe that an animal has developed a concept which, in fact, it has not. For example, Lubow [132] claimed that pigeons could distinguish 'man-made' from 'natural' objects. He used a similar technique to the one used by Herrnstein and Loveland. The slides which depicted 'man-made' scenes were of orchards, cities, roads and so on, whereas the 'natural' ones were of mountains and canyons. However, the 'man-made' slides were both more regular and more complex than the 'natural' slides and so it is quite possible that the pigeons were using regularity or complexity as their cue. This would be quite different from the implication that the pigeons had in some sense realized the difference between landscapes which had been altered by human beings and those which had not.

It would, of course, be possible to answer this objection by increasing the number of slides presented to the pigeons and having some slides which showed simple, irregular man-made scenes and others which showed complex regular 'natural' ones. If the pigeons still discriminated between 'man-made' and 'natural' even when all other cues were confounded, then it would be possible to conclude that they did have the concept of 'man-made'. Designing an experiment to show that an animal does have an abstract concept is, therefore, difficult. But it is not impossible.

Even this very brief account of some of the work that has

been done on the mental experiences which animals might have would be incomplete without some mention of the most dramatic and widely publicised studies of all. Some years ago, a young female chimpanzee named Washoe made history by becoming the first non-human animal to be a competent user of American Sign Language, a gestural language used by deaf people (Gardner and Gardner [66], Fouts [57]). Other chimpanzees and now a gorilla (Patterson [156]) have similarly learnt to make large numbers of word-signs with their hands. They use them at appropriate times and even put them together into novel combinations of their own. Another chimpanzee, Sarah, learnt to 'talk' to her trainers by placing plastic symbols onto a board, each symbol representing a word such as 'give' or 'banana' or 'Sarah' (Premack [159]).

Very far-reaching claims have been made for these chimpanzees, for example, that they understand the symbolic nature of the 'words' in their language and, in the case of Sarah, that she understands the subtleties of grammar. Many workers, including Mouin [149] and Savage – Rumbaugh *et al.* [172] are, however, extremely critical of some of the claims that have been made for Washoe, Sarah and other chimpanzees. They argue that many of the experiments are inadequately controlled or that simpler explanations, such as that the animals are picking up vital clues from their trainers, cannot always be ruled out. We will not go into details here of these controversies, beyond emphasizing that they illustrate the same point as has been stressed throughout this discussion. The criticisms are not that it is unscientific to study the mental abilities of apes. On the contrary, even the criticisms imply that the experiments *could* have been done in such a way that these claims would be substantiated. The chimpanzees may or may not have the abilities that some people think they do. But whether or not they do is open to experimental test.

We can see, then, that many scientists do successfully study at least some mental events in animals. They ask questions about such things as whether animals form concepts and whether they are aware of what they are doing. What is

more, they then go and do experiments. We have also seen
that these experiments have to be very carefully designed and
evaluated. It is very easy to get carried away and read more
into what an animal does than is really there. Animals, like
Clever Hans, may temporarily fool us into believing that they
can do mental arithmetic. Others, by operating a machine,
or using a human tool, may give a superficial impression of
cleverness. As we have seen, this does not mean that animals
cannot understand what they are doing. It just means that we
have to be particularly careful in evaluating the evidence that
they do. But though it is difficult to study mental events in
animals, it is clearly not as impossible as a Behaviourist would
have us believe.

Implications for animal welfare

Griffin [71] has argued that evidence such as that we have
just been discussing makes it very likely that many animals
besides ourselves are conscious and have subjective feelings.
If this is true, it has at least two important implications for
the study of animal welfare. Firstly, it implies that it is
possible to study the mental experiences of animals in a
scientific way. Qualms expressed at the beginning of this
chapter about the feasibility of studying anything as subjective as animal suffering seem to be unfounded. Even if
mental phenomena cannot be studied in exactly the same
ways as behaviour and physiology, we have seen that very
strong indirect evidence can be accumulated about them.
We can acknowledge the truth of the Behaviourists' objection
that mental events are private and cannot be studied
directly, but still not be intimidated by it in practice.

Secondly, this evidence is important because of what it tells
us about animals. Many people may be inclined to change
their attitudes to animals, for example, to killing them or
inflicting pain, if they believe that those animals may be
aware of what is happening to them, may have the capacity
to form concepts and so on. The question "But they're not
very intelligent, are they?" is one with which many people

comfort themselves when drawn into arguments about animal welfare. Their implication seems to be that an animal's welfare does not matter if it is stupid. Some of the studies we have looked at may remove part of that comfort.

We should, nevertheless, beware of assuming either that only intelligent animals suffer or that only the suffering of intelligent animals 'matters' in a moral sense. Singer [185] points out that there is no necessary connection between intelligence and what is of most concern to us in this book, the capacity to suffer. We can see the force of this argument by thinking of a sophisticated, chess-playing computer. We can acknowledge its intelligence without having to believe that it could suffer in any way.

The relationship between an animal's capacity to learn or conceptualize and how we ought to treat it is, then, a complex one. It raises philosophical issues that are largely outside the scope of this book, although we will touch on some of the main problems again in the last chapter. What is much more clear cut, however, is the connection between conscious awareness and the ability to suffer. To say that an animal suffers implies that it is aware of its suffering (that at least will be the assumption made for the rest of the book). Studies such as those we have discussed in this chapter are important because they help us to understand the extent to which an animal is likely to be consciously aware of what is happening to it. This, in turn, will affect our assessment of how much it suffers.

At this point, we can no longer avoid having to define some very difficult terms, beginning with the most difficult of all, 'consciousness'. There are, in fact, many different definitions. Shallice [178], for example, sees it as an information processing device to ensure that an organism does not try to do too many things at once. Humphrey [96] sees it as self-knowledge used to predict the behaviour of other individuals. Hubbard [90] suggests that consciousness has many different elements such as self-awareness (by which he means knowledge of oneself as distinct from other selves), anticipation of the future, ability to manipulate abstract ideas, ability to pay and switch attention and so on.

In trying to apply a definition of consciousness to non-human animals, Hubbard's would seem to be a useful approach, as it emphasizes the complexity of what is usually put under the single heading of 'consciousness'. Different animals might possess some or all of these attributes to different extents, so that it may not be possible to say that an animal is either conscious (possessing all elements) or not (possessing none).

Following Griffin [70], 'awareness' can be taken to mean a whole range of conscious experiences, from toothache to a concept of the universe. In this book, we are particularly concerned with a particular kind of conscious awareness which is referred to as 'suffering'. Here we should attempt a working definition, although it should be stressed that this is in no way a hard and fast or authoritative definition. From now on, 'suffering' will be taken to mean a wide range of unpleasant emotional states. The Brambell Report [17] lists fear, pain, frustration and exhaustion as examples of states of suffering. Such states are the ones with which we will be particularly concerned in this book, largely because they have been most extensively studied in animals. There are, however, other states of suffering, such as those caused by loss of social companions, which also deserve consideration. Indeed, there may be states of suffering which other animals experience and of which we humans have no knowledge.

A major difficulty with any definition of suffering is to decide how much (that is, how intense, or how prolonged) of an unpleasant emotional state constitutes 'suffering'. This is a problem which will be discussed throughout the following chapters. Even at this stage, however, it may be useful to make a distinction between acute pain and longer-lasting suffering. 'Pain', which is discussed more fully in Chapter 3, is usually taken to mean a severe, perhaps transient state, recognizable by positive signs such as screaming and struggling. Other forms of suffering may be less severe at any one time, but continue over long periods of an animal's life.

It is the recognition of these states of suffering which are not acute enough to deserve the name 'pain' that we will be mainly concerned with.

We will be trying to build up a picture of what an animal experiences when it suffers and how it shows what it is feeling. This is a difficult task and there are pitfalls at every step of the way. That is why most of the rest of the book is about the methods which might be our most valuable guides.

3   *Suffering, health and 'productivity'*

We will now begin to explore the possible ways of deciding whether and how much an animal is suffering. The first method we will look at is, in practice, one of the most widely used of all, namely, whether an animal is physically healthy or not. People who have to make laws about the way animals should be kept cannot afford to prevaricate on the question of how we know an animal is suffering in the way that scientists do. They have had to sit down and write precise regulations, and in doing this they have tended to rely heavily on physical health as their standard. Conditions which cause suffering have been seen largely as those in which animals look unhealthy or are liable to injure themselves.

In this chapter, we will look at how valid this criterion is and particularly at the question of whether physical health is the *only* sign of suffering that people need be concerned with. We will see that, although physical health is an important component of any animal's welfare in zoos, circuses, laboratories or wherever animals are kept, it is not sufficient by itself. Physically healthy animals may still suffer mentally. But before we get on to this, we must first make a very clear distinction between the health of an individual animal and the 'productivity' of farm animals. It is very easy to be misled into thinking that these two are the same and that, say, a 'productive' farm must be full of healthy hens all laying large numbers of eggs. Such a confusion is, as we shall see, extremely dangerous, all the more so because it is frequently argued that the high productivity of intensively managed farm animals shows that they cannot possibly be suffering. If animals were distressed, it is argued, they would not give such a good yield. The very success of intensive methods is sometimes seen as a vindication of the way the animals are treated.

To see the fallacy in this argument, we must look in rather more detail at the way commercial interests affect the welfare of individual animals.

Commercial interests and animal interests

First of all, it is necessary to be quite clear what is meant by the two terms physical health and productivity. 'Physical health' is usually taken to mean a generally good condition shown by such things as a sleek coat or plumage, bright eyes and alertness. In this chapter, ill-health will be used only to refer to clear departures from good health which are readily detectable by looking at the animal. More subtle physiological changes which may occur without any obvious effects on the animal's external appearance are discussed in Chapter 5. Of course, the precise signs of health and disease will vary from species to species, but for each one it is usually possible to draw up a list of indications of major disturbances of health. For example, in cattle, the signs of ill-health given in the Welfare Codes [27] include "listlessness, loss of appetite, fall in milk-yield, not cudding, discharge from the nostrils or eyes, persistent coughing, swollen joints, lameness and scouring". Similar lists can be, and in many cases have been, drawn up for other animals.

'Productivity', on the other hand, has economic overtones. It refers to the commercial profit that can be made from an animal. It can be measured either at the level of the individual animal or that of a whole farm unit. We will discuss these separately as they have rather different consequences for the welfare of the animal.

As Murphy [151] points out, even looking at the productivity of individual animals is not straightforward, because productivity is measured in so many different ways. It is sometimes measured as how efficient that animal is at converting food into meat. It is sometimes measured as the number of young a sow has in each litter or the number of litters she has each year. It may also be measured as the number of eggs a hen lays each year or how much food is needed to produce one egg and so on. This plethora of definitions makes it quite difficult to establish whether there is any connection between productivity and welfare. For example, a sow which produces a large number of piglets in each litter (and is in this sense productive), may eat prodigious quantities of food (and in this sense not be productive). Different productivity measures may therefore not correlate very well.

Even if we pick on one measure of productivity, such as how much food an animal needs to gain a certain amount of weight, there are still problems in establishing what this means for the welfare of the animal. Take as an example a very 'productive' turkey which ate relatively little food, but put on weight very fast. This might be because it was kept indoors in a confined space and was unable to exercise. Alternatively, it might be because it was free of parasites and spent less time trying to escape than a less productive turkey. Clearly, depending on which of these were the case, we might draw quite different conclusions about the physical health and general welfare of the turkey. As Murphy [151] emphasizes, we cannot therefore assume that there is any connection between productivity and welfare until we have looked in more detail at the reasons behind the productivity.

If productivity, however defined, of individual animals is an unreliable indicator of their welfare, productivity of whole farm units is even more so. Even if we could establish a connection between an animal's health and some measure of its productivity, we would still be up against some harsh economic facts. Profits in agriculture are not made by setting up conditions in which each *individual* animal is maximally productive, or even maximally healthy. Rather, profits are made by running a whole farm unit efficiently which depends not just upon the animals, but also on the initial investment in housing and the considerable feed and labour costs once it is running (McBride [133]).

The complexity of what goes into the making of profits in agriculture has some very important consequences in practice. There may be some circumstances in which it is actually more profitable for a farm unit as a whole if the animals are kept in conditions in which their individual productivity is less than maximal. Economies of space, for example, putting more hens into a battery cage, may lower individual productivity, but enable larger numbers of animals to be kept in the same area. This may more than compensate for the losses on each individual (Ewer [54]). Laying the egg is only one stage in the long process of getting eggs into the shops. The eggs have to be collected without too much wastage and dirt; birds have to be fed and inspected; and the labour to do these things is expensive. Systems of keeping hens in which they lay large numbers of eggs will not be economically viable if they fail in one of these other respects. Economies of labour or housing may outweigh the advantages of a small increase in numbers of eggs laid by each hen.

In the most intensive units of broiler chickens, a single man may look after 20 000 or more birds at a time (Donaldson and Donaldson [40]). In such units, a single bird makes only a minor contribution to the final profit. Considerable losses, of growth rate, food use and even death in some animals can be tolerated before it becomes worthwhile to employ more men or to increase the space allowed to each bird.

Similarly, the very considerable initial investment that is necessary for some kinds of pig housing may force farmers to buy cheaper accommodation. This may mean that each individual pig will be less productive (it may need more food, for example, to achieve the same body weight because it is colder) than more expensively housed pigs. But in the long run, it makes better economic sense to sacrifice productivity of the individual animals for the capital saved on the initial outlay of the whole unit.

Wastage of food is another factor which may make one

system of management more productive than another, without any obvious improvement in the physical welfare of the animals kept in them. In some intensive units, for example, there may be many pigs rooting over the same area and picking up food which has spilled onto the floor. Because the food is not wasted, the unit will be more productive (in terms of the ratio of the food supplied to the live weight gain) than a less intensive system in which a lot of food is wasted (Ewbank [50, 51]). But it is clearly possible that the physical state of the pigs crowded together and eating food which had dropped onto the floor would be worse than the ones given more room.

The possibility of a split between the conditions which are commercially best for the farmer and those which favour the health of the individual animal becomes greater the more animals that comprise the total unit. The smaller the proportion of the profit that is represented by one animal, the less that animal, in an economic sense, matters. On a small farm, loss of production or death of a single animal will have a much greater impact than in a large unit of hundreds or thousands of animals. Such large units are becoming more and more of a common feature of modern farming. In Britain, for example, more than half the entire output from agriculture in 1977 came from only 14.5% of the farm holdings (Central Office of Information [25]). The trend towards larger units is particularly apparent in the keeping of poultry where about 75% of all broilers are in so-called 'flocks' of 50 000 or more and over 90% of all laying hens are in battery cages and owned by some 21% of producers (COI [25]).

The total number of animals involved in the agricultural industry also indicates how relatively insignificant one animal is. About 300 million broilers, nearly 3 million cattle, over 10 million sheep and some 14 million pigs are slaughtered each year in Britain alone (UFAW report [204]).

An enormous amount of effort has gone into increasing the efficiency of this industry. The rising costs of land, feedstuff and labour have meant that the most efficient farming

practices are those which take up as little space as possible
and use labour sparingly (Ewer [54]). It has been found that
by keeping animals such as pigs indoors all their lives and
never letting them get too hot or too cold, they will put on
weight without requiring as much food as if they were
outside. By having animals fed automatically on conveyor
belts, labour costs can be cut and one man can look after
large numbers of animals. By careful breeding, it is possible
to create new genetic strains of animals that grow and lay
eggs even better than the traditional breeds.

As a result of all these factors, agriculture has shown a
quite dramatic increase in productivity over recent years. For
instance, since 1954, egg production per hen has increased
from an average of 161 eggs per year to about 230, with some
strains managing over 260 (Midgley [146]; COI [25]).
Furthermore, a dozen eggs can now be produced on about
half the food that was needed in the early part of this century.

Within this vast efficient industry, one animal is a very
small cog. For this reason, the productivity of modern
farming says very little about the welfare of the individual
animal. It says little about its physical health, let alone its
mental welfare. Of course, if the physical health of animals
deteriorated too far, profits would fall, so that there is some
kind of ultimate limit on the conditions in which animals can
be kept commercially. But before this limit is reached, it may
still be profitable to keep them in suboptimal conditions as
far as their own physical health is concerned, as Ewer [54]
and Harrison [76], amongst others, have emphasized.

It would be quite wrong to give the impression that
intensively kept farm animals are generally in bad health and
that farmers are only out for profit. On the contrary, Ewbank
[50] considers that the standards of health in intensively
managed animals are generally very high. Harrison [76]
reports the result of a poll which suggests that most farmers
are very concerned for the welfare of their animals. But the
point that is being stressed is that productivity is no
guarantee of the yield and certainly not of the well-being of
single animals within them, particularly when the units are

large and intensive ones. This is quite separate from the question of whether individual animals actually are more productive and healthy under one system or another. They may or may not be, but this has to be decided by subsequent investigation of the animals themselves, not from looking at a balance sheet.

Having made the distinction between the productivity of a farm considered as a unit and the state of the individual within that unit, let us now focus attention on the individual. It is, after all, individuals that have subjective experiences and individuals that have the potential for suffering. It is, therefore, the welfare of individual animals, not species or farms with which we are basically concerned.

Suffering and ill-health

Bad health and debilitating illness are amongst the major causes of suffering in human beings. For most people, the possession of all their faculties and the absence of painful disease are important to their general well-being. It is widely accepted that the same is true of other species. For example, Thorpe [197] stated that animals would clearly suffer if kept in conditions in which they were made physically deformed. The Brambell Committee [17] pointed to disease as a very major cause of suffering in animals. And the Welfare Codes [27] issued by the UK Government emphasize that priority should be given to ensuring that animals are kept in good health and to treating any signs of disease.

As outlined earlier in this chapter, ill-health is being used here to refer only to gross and obvious disturbances of health, more subtle changes being discussed in Chapter 5. Because of this somewhat extreme definition, it seems reasonable to argue, as many others have, that ill-health clearly indicates suffering. If an animal is diseased or shows signs of ill-health such as those mentioned earlier in the chapter, then that alone would seem sufficient to say that the animal is suffering. There is almost no need to employ any other methods for recognizing suffering at all.

Injury is another potential source of suffering. It is, however, impossible to make a blanket statement to the effect that all injury causes suffering because this is clearly not the case from human experience. Thus, as Melzack [140] documents, people can have extensive injuries (for instance, soldiers wounded in battle) and yet report little or no pain. Conversely, people complaining of severe pain can baffle their doctors because they have no injury or tissue damage. Thus pain seems to have two components: the perception of actual or threatened damage to the body and the unpleasant and highly aversive subjective qualities that usually go with this (Casey [24]; Mersky & Spear [144]; Mountcastle [150]).

How can we recognize when injury is giving rise to the subjective experience of pain? There are two sources of evidence, physiological and behavioural. It is widely accepted (e.g. Keele and Smith [106]; Kerr and Casey [108]) that the physiological mechanisms of pain perception are similar in humans and other animals. The difficulty is that the physiological basis of pain is still not well understood in any species so that it is not as easy as it might seem to know when an organism is in pain from its physiology alone. For example, it is known that there are small diameter nerve fibres which are found all over the body and which respond to painful stimuli (Kerr and Casey [108]). But these do not join up into discrete bundles which can be examined for pain messages in the same way as, say, the optic nerve can be examined for visual ones. The situation is further complicated by the existence of nerve fibres which come *out* from the brain and affect the extent to which painful stimuli are allowed to travel up the spinal cord and hence the extent to which the organism ultimately feels pain (Melzack and Wall [141]).

Because the physiology of pain is still so problematical, behavioural evidence is perhaps more convincing. Although there is some controversy over exactly which behavioural measures are the most reliable indicators of mild pain (Kerr and Casey [108]), most people agree that the signs of intense pain in both human and non-human animals are unmistakable.

They include squealing, struggling, convulsions and so on (e.g. Littlewood Report [128]).

It is clear, then, that if animals show gross disturbances of health or injuries leading to pain, they can reasonably be said to suffer. What is not so clear, however, is what we can conclude if the animal's physical health is good at least by the rather crude criteria we have discussed so far, and if there are no signs of painful injuries. As we will see in the next section, there are reasons for thinking that not all mental suffering is necessarily reflected in such obvious signs of physical debilitation.

Limitations of physical health as a measure of suffering

Bertrand Russell began his book *The Conquest of Happiness* [167] with the bland statement that "Animals are happy so long as they have health and enough to eat". We will now look at the evidence which suggests that this is much too simple a view.

The Brambell Committee [17] pointed out that if the period of suffering were relatively short, it might have no long term effects on the animal's physical health. Nevertheless they believed that the suffering could be very intense while it lasted. When animals are captured or transported, for example, this does not always affect their physical health in overt ways. However, this may well be because there is no time for serious health defects to make themselves shown. The animal may soon be released or the journey may soon be over. One reason for supposing that, given time, the animal's health would be affected is that it is often possible to detect physiological disturbances such as changed hormone levels which, as we will discuss more fully in Chapter 5, may be the precursors of ill-health. Sometimes, indeed, capture and transport, do cause weight loss, bruising, injury and physical deterioration so severe as to lead to death (Hails [72]). At the same time, and often before these overt signs of suffering are occurring, physiological changes such as hormone levels and the ammonia content of muscle are also apparent. The existence of similar changes in animals whose external condition is apparently adequate by the criteria we have so far discussed has lead to the idea that these physiological disturbances should be regarded as signs of suffering in their own right. At the very least they appear to be early warning signs of suffering yet to come, and we will explore what they tell us about animal suffering more fully in Chapter 5.

So the existence of physiological disturbances when, on the surface, the animal is apparently healthy, is one reason for believing that physical health is not the only yardstick we need for measuring animal suffering. This may be a particularly important consideration when evaluating agricultural practices that involve very young animals. If the animals are reared quickly and then slaughtered, there may not be time for any pathological symptoms to appear. Broiler chickens, for example, are now usually killed when they are 7 – 8 weeks old, having gained over 43 times their weight at hatching in their short life. When they are fully grown, the birds have only $0.5 - 0.75$ ft^2 floor space each, but they live only a matter of days under these conditions before being slaughtered (Sainsbury [171]). Pigs are killed when they are 15 – 30 weeks old, and veal calves when they are about 12 weeks (Wilson [207]). There may not, therefore, be time for 'suffering' to be shown in actual damage to health. At least, this is a possibility that cannot be ruled out without first looking at other methods for assessing suffering.

There is another reason why physical health should not be too readily equated with the absence of suffering. This is that even healthy animals may sometimes show highly 'abnormal' behaviour which appears to be the result of restriction or crowding. Zoo animals, for instance, are medically well cared for, well fed and protected from the elements yet may show bizarre behaviour patterns such as pacing backwards and forwards, bobbing up and down, masturbation, self-mutilation and so on. The interpretation of such abnormal behaviour and what it tells us about animal suffering is the subject of Chapter 6. For the moment, we will take the occurrence of such behaviour in apparently healthy animals as an indication that it is important to look beyond physical health to be sure that an animal is in a state of well-being.

We can conclude this chapter by stressing once again that physical health is a very important factor in the welfare of any animal. If we want to know whether an animal is suffering, the first question we should ask is about its health and condition. We should, however, be careful to distinguish 'health' from 'productivity', which has economic overtones. As we have seen, 'productivity' is an unreliable indicator of either physical or mental health, particularly where it is applied to whole groups of animals rather than to individuals.

The clear-cut disturbances of physical health which we have been considering are generally agreed to be signs of severe or prolonged suffering. But they may be relatively insensitive indicators of short-term or less acute suffering. It takes relatively little time for an animal to feel pain or to suffer. But it may take much longer for its health to be affected. Physiological and behavioural abnormalities in apparently healthy animals suggest that we should try to find more sensitive measures of suffering. These we will discuss in subsequent chapters.

4   *Suffering and the 'unnatural' life*

One of the things that disturbs people most about animals in captivity is that their lives are 'unnatural'. They cannot move around freely as they would in the wild and, if the animals are kept in very small, bare cages, there is much behaviour that they are completely prevented from doing. So the most obvious method for assessing suffering to consider next is the extent to which an animal is able to perform the behaviour patterns typical of its species.

In this chapter, we will look at the idea that wild animals or animals that have been in captivity and have then escaped, might provide a standard against which the welfare of the captive ones could be measured. Our main task will be to try to see how valid it is to assume that animals which cannot perform their species-typical behaviour patterns suffer as a result. By the end of the chapter it should be clear that although differences between the behaviour of captive and wild animals are instructive, they do not in themselves provide evidence that the captive ones are suffering. An 'unnatural' life is not necessarily one of suffering any more than a life in the wild is necessarily free from it. It will be apparent that there are several arguments here, all interwoven with each other and we will have to be careful not to confuse romantic notions about Nature and Freedom with scientific evidence on genetics, development and what happens if animals are prevented from behaving in certain ways. But before we get on to these arguments, let us look at the more positive side of using wild animals to help us in the task of identifying animal suffering and look at the ways that have been suggested for implementing this idea.

'Natural' behaviour and welfare

There is undoubtedly something very attractive about the idea of wild animals roaming freely in their natural environment, able to feed, mate and bear their young without human interference. This is the condition in which they have evolved and many people believe that this is the 'right' way for animals to live. The conditions in which animals are kept by human beings can, to such people, be judged by how close they are to the wild habitat and the extent to which the animals are able to behave in a natural way. Small cages and crowded conditions such as those seen in some petshops, zoos and farms come out particularly badly in their view as they are very different from anything the animals would experience in nature.

Such ideas are very widely held and have even become written into laws governing the way animals should be kept. The Federal German Parliament, for instance, passed a very far-reaching animal welfare law in 1972 (The Animal Protection Act) which required that anyone keeping an animal should "provide accommodation which takes account of its natural behaviour" (Ray and Scott [162]).

The most persuasive scientific arguments in favour of using the naturalness of behaviour as a criterion of welfare were put forward by Thorpe [195, 196]. He argued that ways of keeping animals that prevented them from expressing their "natural instinctive urges" should be condemned as they undoubtedly caused suffering. He went on to describe the 'natural' behaviour of all the most intensively kept farm animals, chickens, pigs, sheep and cattle, defining 'natural' as the behaviour of the presumed wild ancestors in each case. Thorpe made the important point that all these animals have highly developed social behaviour and that one of the main effects of their confinement is to disrupt their social interactions. Calves are taken from their mothers within the first 3 days of life, for example, and then confined on their own. Laying hens are kept in small cages in very close proximity to other birds. He believed that if animals were unable to move around freely, then they would also suffer. The Brambell Committee [17] agreed with Thorpe and concluded: "The degree to which the behavioural urges of the animal are frustrated under the particular conditions of the confinement must be a major consideration in determining its acceptability or otherwise" (p. 13).

Thorpe later [197] took his ideas even further. He argued that it is possible to rank the degree of suffering imposed on an animal according to which behaviour patterns it is unable to perform. The greatest suffering, he argued, is caused by the suppression of those actions which the animal would perform most frequently under more natural conditions. In the case of poultry he lists feeding, locomotion, preening, social responses and sleeping as being the most frequent behaviour patterns, prevention of which he therefore saw as causing the most suffering to the birds.

The idea that an animal which is unable to show natural behaviour patterns is suffering is a very important one. In order to make it quite clear what the arguments in favour and against it are, we will take one specific example, the comparison between the domestic chicken and the species which is generally thought to be its ancestor, the Red Junglefowl (Beebe [11]; Delacour [39]). Similar comparisons could be made between any other species and its wild counterparts, but chickens illustrate the problems involved in a particularly acute form. They have been bred by human beings over many generations and they are frequently kept in conditions which are very different from the Asian jungles of their ancestors. Some animals, such as wild animals in zoos, share with them the unnaturalness of their environment, but are genetically similar to truly wild animals. Others, such as dogs, share with them the long history of artificial breeding, but do not have such severe restrictions on their behaviour. So as a domesticated animal in one of the most unnatural environments that could be devised, battery-kept hens enable us to discuss all aspects of the 'natural behaviour' criterion.

Straight away, it is obvious that many features of junglefowl life are quite impossible in the crowded conditions of modern intensive farms. Outside the breeding season, wild junglefowl (which look very like some breeds of bantams) usually move around in flocks of one cock and a small harem of 2 − 5 hens (Collias and Collias [29]; Collias and Sachnae [30]; Johnson [104]). They are very shy and wary and they can fly very well. In the heat of midday, they roost together in clumps of thorny bamboo. During the breeding season, the hens separate and move off on their own to rear their chicks, choosing nesting sites well hidden from view.

In battery cages, in stark contrast, hens are forced into continuous close proximity to other hens. They cannot flap their wings or move more than a few steps. They lay their eggs standing up as they have no nests. Since the floors of the cages are made of wire, the birds cannot dustbathe although they may 'go through the motions', even with no dust. And they have nowhere to roost.

A considerable proportion of the 'natural' behaviour of the fowl cannot, therefore, be performed by hens in battery cages and, on these grounds, battery cages would be said to cause suffering. But the conclusion that hens suffer because they cannot behave as junglefowl do makes a number of assumptions, each of which is questionable. The first is that there are no significant genetic or environmentally produced differences between the wild and domesticated forms. The second is that if an animal behaves differently from its wild counterpart, that shows that it is suffering. The third is that wild animals do not experience suffering. These are the same assumptions that are made whenever the behaviour of any wild animal is proposed as a standard for welfare, and do not just apply to chickens and junglefowl. So, because of their general importance, we will now discuss each of the three assumptions in turn. The arguments are intended to apply to all animals, but we will return from time to time to the specific example of the junglefowl when it illustrates a particular point.

Are there differences between wild and domesticated animals?

In this section, we will first look at the possible genetic

changes that have occurred in animals as a result of domestication and then later at the environmental factors which may make them different from wild animals too.

We know that for thousands of years, human beings have been tinkering with animal genetics. They probably began with dogs over 12 000 years ago (Davis and Valla [36]; Protsch and Berger [160]). They then moved on to goats between 7000 and 8000 B.C. and to sheep a thousand or so years later (Zeuner [212]). By 2500 B.C., there were already several distinctive types of cattle, so that cattle breeding must have begun much earlier than this, perhaps about 7000 B.C. (Reed [163]). Pigs have been domesticated for over 7000 years (Signoret *et al.* [184]) and chickens for over 4000 years (Wood-Gush [208]). The first recorded use of pigeons to carry messages was in the reign of Rameses III in Egypt in 1204 B.C. (Hyams [98]).

Most of these are conservative estimates as they are based on archaeological evidence which can only show that domestication had already occurred by a particular date. The true beginnings of domestication are probably much earlier. In any case, long before human beings had completely domesticated their animals in the sense of having full control over their maintenance and breeding, they could have affected them genetically. By protecting or feeding semi-wild animals, they would help some animals to breed better than others. As Spurway [190] pointed out, even a small bias in this way would have produced animals that were more inbred or more outbred than before and which therefore possessed previously rare combinations of genes. For this reason, Spurway maintained that even animals bred in zoos, whose parents or grandparents might have been completely wild, will be genetically different from any wild animal.

But at least for dogs, cattle, pigs, sheep, goats and domestic fowl, we are seeing animals after thousands of generations of human influence over their breeding, at first tentative and partial, later on controlled and directed. Domestic animals have diversified into hundreds of varieties, some of them grotesque like pouter pigeons, others useful like high-yielding dairy cows. All domestic animals will interbreed freely with their wild counterparts (Siegel [183] so that domestication is, by the standards of geological time, a minor evolutionary event. Domestication has nevertheless resulted in some quite major changes, affecting many different aspects of animals' lives. We have to consider the possibility that some animals are now so changed, so selected for the conditions laid down by human beings, that their 'natural' environments are no longer the jungles, woods or plains that were the homes of their ancestors in the distant past.

To illustrate this, let us go back to the example of the junglefowl and see what sort of changes have occurred. Hutt [97] made a direct comparison between White Leghorn hens and Red Junglefowl hens, all hatched in incubators and all kept under the same conditions. His junglefowl laid an average of 62 eggs a year and while this was considerably more than they would lay in the wild, it was nothing like the average of 181 eggs of the White Leghorns. One of the reasons for this difference is that White Leghorns are less likely to go broody (Bowman [15]). In nature, a junglefowl will lay a clutch of eggs and then stop laying to incubate and rear the chicks. But going broody under modern farm conditions is just a nuisance as it prevents the birds from getting on with the serious business of laying more eggs. So one of the effects of breeding for 'laying more eggs' has been to select birds which are least likely to go broody.

Another reason why White Leghorns are better layers is that they mature earlier than junglefowl (Bowman [15]) and can therefore start laying sooner. Selection for egg-laying seems also to have had some quite surprising side effects too. In a number of cases it has affected how aggressive the birds are. Sometimes it has resulted in the birds becoming more aggressive because these are the ones that can best gain access to food and water which in turn enables them to lay more eggs (James and Foenander [101]; Lowry and Abplanalp [131]). At other times, it is the less aggressive birds which lay the most eggs (Frankham and Weiss [59a]). Unexpected changes in the appearance of the comb may occur in strains selected solely for their ability to lay eggs (Frankham and Doornenbal [59b]).

A good egg layer is therefore not just a junglefowl which lays a lot of eggs, because artificial selection does not act on a single characteristic and leave all the rest alone. By selecting for egg-laying, people have altered the parental behaviour (e.g. broodiness), rate of development and such things as the aggressive behaviour of chickens, because many of these are directly related to the character they are interested in. They have also unwittingly affected characters such as comb shape which have nothing obvious to do with laying eggs, but which have been 'dragged along' in the process.

This brings us to another reason for being cautious about comparing wild and domesticated animals. Considerable genetic differences exist among domesticated animals themselves, both in what they look like and what they do. Domestic animals do not form genetically similar groups all behaving in the same way. They differ from each other in almost every characteristic one can think of, including how aggressive they are, how successful they are at mating, how easily they learn and so on (for a review, see Siegel [183]). There are some bizarre examples of how far this genetic variation has gone. Selection for broad-breasted turkeys, for instance, has had the effect of producing birds which find difficulty in balancing, to such an extent that when they try to mate, they fall over. Consequently, the best table birds have to be propagated by artificial insemination.

The genetic differences among domestic animals mean that neat and tidy comparisons with wild animals are simply not possible. There is no such thing as 'the pig' or 'the chicken'. It depends on which breed is being considered. Hughes [92] believes that, for the domestic hen, the behavioural differences, between modern broiler strains and modern egg-laying strains are greater than those that exist between a 'primitive' breed such as Brown Leghorns and ancestral junglefowl. He argues that there appear to have been as many genetic changes in chickens over the last 100 years as in all the preceding 4500 years put together. In other words, controlled programmes of intensive artifical selection have had very major effects in a comparatively short time.

We have, then, to be very careful in generalizing from one domestic strain to another and from any one of these to the wild ancestors. It might be thought that, if there are such dangers in using truly wild animals as models of our domestic ones, the obvious thing to do would be to study feral populations, that is domestic animals which have run wild. This approach has indeed been very fruitful. For example, there is a population of over a million feral pigs running loose in the South-eastern United States, probably derived from animals that escaped from an expedition led by Fernando de Soto in 1539 (Hanson and Karstad [73]). Radio-tracking of these animals (e.g. Kurz and Marchinton [123]) has revealed a considerable amount about their social behaviour, how many animals there are in a group and so on. The Soay sheep of St Kilda are a free-living population of primitive European sheep, probably resembling those brought to Britain by farmers in prehistoric times (Jewell and others [103]). There are numerous populations of feral chickens, including one studied by McBride *et al.* [134] on an uninhabited coral island off the coast of Australia. These birds had been introduced there about the end of the last century and their behaviour turned out to be very similar to that of truly wild junglefowl.

One of the most interesting experiments on feral animals involved a deliberate release of domestic hens onto a Scottish island. Wood-Gush and Duncan [211] found that when they first did this, almost all the birds were killed immediately, falling victim to mink which had managed to swim across from the mainland. Wood-Gush and Duncan were determined, however, to try and get a population established. So they gave their next batch of chickens special 'commando training' before releasing them. This was successful and the birds evaded the mink for quite a time. What was particularly striking about these birds was the way they chose inaccessible and extremely well-hidden nest sites and the wariness with which they approached their nests (Duncan *et al.* [48]).

But studies of feral animals, too, have their drawbacks. The 'wild' habitat into which animals escape or are released may be very different from their natural home; compare a windy Scottish island with a tropical Asian jungle. This means that feral populations may be subject to selection pressures unique to themselves. They may become genetically distinct over the years, both from animals that are completely under human control and from truly wild ancestral populations as well. What is more, feral animals differ in another important respect from captive ones. They are born and reared in conditions which are totally unlike those of captivity. And as we will now see, what an animal experiences during its lifetime, particularly when it is young, can have a very great and lasting effect upon its behaviour and on its likes and dislikes. For example, puppies raised together but out of sight of human beings for 14 weeks become very shy of people and are to all intents and purposes wild animals (Freedman *et al.* [62]). Even very subtle environmental factors can have far-reaching effects. Pfaffenberger *et al.* [158] found that dogs which are best at guiding blind people are ones which have spent a good part of their puppyhood in a family of children. Dogs left in kennels after the age of 3 months tended to become nervous and unsatisfactory even as pets, let alone as guide dogs. A family with several children seemed to provide a better environment than a family with only one (Pfaffenberger *et al.* [158]. Being able to run free in the countryside also seemed to affect a dog's later success at being a guide dog, particularly the extent to which it would disobey orders which would endanger the blind master. City dogs which had never had the experience of roaming in open country did not seem to do as well as guide dogs, even with 'city' hazards such as manholes.

With other animals, too, early experience is an important modifier of their behaviour. Newly hatched birds such as ducklings will follow very unbird-like objects, such as human beings, flashing lights or boxes and form strong attachments to them if they see them at certain critical times of their lives (Immelmann [100]; Sluckin [187]). Although this 'imprinting' is not as indelible as was once thought (Cooke and McNally [32]; Schutz [175]) it may nevertheless influence the birds' choice of a mate when they become adult. Contact with human beings may also affect what zoo animals regard as a suitable mate. This may be inconvenient if it is an emu that approaches its keeper as if he were a female of its own species, but positively dangerous if it happens with a moose (Hediger [78]). Kittens play differently depending on how they are reared (Bateson [10]) and the way a mother rhesus monkey treats her baby depends on what she herself experienced when an infant (Sackett and Ruppenthal [170]).

Experience during early life might significantly affect the degree of similarity between domestic and wild animals by determining the kind of environment the respective animals prefer to live in. Lorenz [129] pointed out the importance of familiar surroundings for animals and once again we can turn to chickens for a specific example of this. Hens which had been living for some time in battery cages were found to prefer these cages even to an outside run with grass when they were first offered a free choice between the two (Dawkins [37, 38]) Although there are problems of interpreting just what such choices mean (and we will discuss these fully in Chapter 7), this study does suggest that what an animal is used to could have a significant effect on what the animal regarded as the most desirable environment to live in. At the present moment, we know relatively little about developmental factors in animal welfare. 'Battery hens', for instance, are usually regarded as a uniform group, but their responses may well be different depending on whether they have lived all their lives in battery cages or whether they have enjoyed the relative freedom of deep litter houses before being put into the cages. The degree to which they suffer may similarly be radically altered by what they have experienced before. We simply do not know. But in view of the known effects of early experience in other aspects of animals' lives, this would seem to be a fruitful area for research.

Enough has been said by now to make it clear that the comparison between wild and domestic animals is not straightforward. Selection (over thousands of years) and experience (over the lifetime of the individual) could potentially bring about major differences between the two. The existence of great genetic and environmentally produced diversity among domestic animals should make us wary of generalizing from one domestic strain to another, let alone from any of them to completely wild animals.

Before attempting to use wild animals as a standard for the welfare of captive ones, we have, therefore, to *find out* whether there are genetic or environmental differences between the two. The point of this section has been to argue that we cannot assume that there are none.

Do animals suffer if they cannot behave naturally?

A second and perhaps more questionable assumption behind the idea of using wild animals as standards for welfare is that animals suffer if they are not able to do everything that is in the repertoire of their species. Such is the power of words that if we talk about 'suppression of instinctive drives', we give a vivid picture of a thwarted animal prevented from doing what it desperately wants to. There are overtones of suffering in the very words that are used. But if we use different words and say simply that there is some behaviour which is seen in wild animals but not in captive ones, then it becomes easier to separate in our minds the description of what the differences are, from the question of whether suffering is caused by them.

Perry [157] has stressed that there is no necessary connection between an animal being prevented from doing a behaviour and whether or not that animal suffers. A simple example will illustrate this point. Domestic animals show, on the whole, much less escape and anti-predator behaviour than wild ones. But it would clearly be wrong to jump to the conclusion that domestic animals suffer through not being able to express their anti-predator behaviour. In fact, starting with the observation that human beings protect their animals from many of their natural enemies, it would be possible to argue in two completely opposite directions. One argument would be that animals protected from their predators must be better off, since the fear aroused by having to escape and the injuries that might be sustained, cause them to suffer considerably. Captivity serves in this case to protect the animal and reduce its risk of injury. Hence this line of reasoning would lead to the conclusion that the reduction of anti-predator behaviour in domestic animals is an indication of the benefit they derive and suggests that they are, at least in this respect, less likely to suffer.

The diametrically opposite argument goes like this. If animals do not have the opportunity to perform behaviour which they would do in the wild, then they suffer, if only from boredom. In support of this idea there is evidence that some animals seek out stimulation even when it puts them in danger. Kruuk [121], for example, describes how some African mammals will move in so close to their predators that they get killed by them.

Kruuk also observed a similar phenomenon in herring gulls and lesser black-backed gulls [122], both of which will approach predators such as foxes. He found that they were particularly likely to come close to a model of a predator (a stuffed fox, stoat or hedgehog) if it had a dead gull lying beside it. But, having once seen one of these models with a dead gull, the gulls then kept a much greater distance away from that predator when they next saw it. Kruuk believes that they learn about the dangers of a gull-killing predator by deliberately seeking it out, even though this might mean some risk at the time.

Humphrey [95] describes another example of animals putting themselves into a frightening situation. He trained monkeys to press a lever to be able to see films or photographs. Some of these pictures produced signs of acute fear in the monkeys (ears back, urinating, etc.) the first time they saw them. Yet the monkeys still continued to press the lever to see the same pictures, which can consequently be referred to as 'horror films'. So animals do not always seek a quiet life. They may put themselves in situations which evoke fear and which may be dangerous to them. It might be argued that by depriving captive animals of these opportunities, they suffer. We have arrived at the opposite conclusion to the one above.

This is not an argument one way or the other on the question of whether less anti-predator behaviour means less or more suffering. It simply illustrates that by starting with the observation that there exist differences between the behaviour of wild and domestic animals, we could argue either that the domestic animals were better off or that the wild ones were. The fact that it is possible to arrive at such totally different conclusions shows that there is nothing in these differences *as such* which tells us about animal suffering. The evidence for suffering, if it exists, must come from other sources.

What do we know about the effects of not performing certain species-typical behaviour patterns? It is very difficult to make generalizations, because the effects tend to be very different depending on the particular behaviour that is being considered. For example, the longer an animal is prevented from feeding or drinking, the more likely it becomes to feed and drink when given the opportunity to do so (Toates and Archer [200]). But the same is not necessarily true of other behaviour patterns such as fighting. Heiligenberg and Kramer [79] found that the longer a cichlid fish (*Haplochromis*) had been without fighting, the *less* likely it was to fight when given the chance to do so. Heiligenberg and Kramer argued that this difference in the effects of preventing feeding and preventing aggression makes functional sense since the longer an animal has been without feeding, the nearer it comes to dying of starvation and the greater the priority it should give to eating. But the longer the fish has been without fighting, the more likely it is that there are no rivals around and the less priority it should give to chasing them off.

Houston and McFarland [88] have suggested that it may be possible to classify the effects of not performing different actions in terms of what they call 'behavioural resilience'. 'Resilience' is their measure of the cost to the animal of not doing one of its natural behaviour patterns, where 'cost' refers to damaging effects on survival and reproduction. They have also argued informally that 'resilience' might be a valuable concept in the assessment of animal welfare as it would given an indication of the relative importance to the animal of each of the actions in its repertoire.

At the moment, this approach is in its infancy and we can say with confidence only that there is considerable diversity in the effects of not performing an action. It seems likely that this would be reflected in a similar diversity of effects on the animal's subjective feelings. Lack of opportunity for behaving in certain ways may sometimes result in extreme suffering but in other cases it might be positively pleasurable. The mere existence of differences between wild and captive animals does not enable us to say which of these is true. In the following chapters we will be looking at some of the physiological signs which might give us a clue.

Is a 'natural' life free from suffering?

Using wild animals as a standard of welfare makes the implicit assumption that the wild ones are not suffering. This assumption is the most questionable of all the ones we have considered. Wild animals are continually exposed to hazards such as disease and predation. Darwin [34], in a letter to J. D. Hooker wrote: "What a book a devil's chaplain might write on the clumsy, wasteful, blundering, low and horribly cruel works of nature!"

As a result, captive animals may often be healthier, and in this sense, better off than wild ones (Russell and Burch [168]). Injured animals in captivity, for instance, can be recognized and treated quickly, whereas a wild one may be left to a slow lingering death.

The high chances of death in wild animals illustrates the

fact that they are continuously exposed to danger. Lack [125] came to the startling conclusion that the average adult song-bird such as a robin or song sparrow, which might live for 11 or so years in captivity, lives only 1 − 2 years in the wild. Even this over-estimates the life expectancy at hatching, for a great many birds die before they reach adulthood. Lack expresses this point vividly: "We ourselves would be shocked if half our friends died each year, and in fact mankind experiences a death-rate of this magnitude only under unusual circumstances, such as the Black Death in 1348 or in some of the actions by Commando units in the late war. But in wild song-birds this is the normal state of affairs" (p. 93).

Not only is life in the wild short and hazardous, especially for young animals, but the method of death may also cause suffering. In the Serengeti National Park in Tanzania, large numbers of animals (particularly wildebeest) have been found dead and dying, probably of starvation (Kruuk [121]).

Death by predation may be shorter but it may well be painful. Spotted hyenas, for instance, do not have a specific killing bite or method of quickly killing their prey. Instead, they simply kill their victim by eating it (Kruuk [121]). Kruuk's own description of this is vivid: "It is rare that the victim puts up any significant active defence: usually a group of hyenas has no difficulty in attacking the hind-quarters of an animal, biting its loins and anal region, and, if there are many hyenas, also the throat and chest. They tear chunks away of skin, muscles and intestines, and this will bring down the victim and kill it in anything from 1 to 13 m".

Many people will still argue, however, that in spite of all the dangers, it is still 'better' for animals to be free and subject to natural hazards than to have to endure the confinement of farm or laboratory. Clearly, though, we have to be very careful over what is meant by the word 'better' in this context. If better does not mean better protected against predators, better fed and so on, it is important to say what it does mean. Otherwise we fall into the trap of thinking that a natural life is better simply because it seems more romantic to us from the outside.

Sheep, for instance, are often thought to lead romantic lives, free from suffering, because they wander freely on hillsides, unconstrained by cages and other inventions of modern farming. But Ewbank [53] argues that mountain sheep in winter probably suffer more than many animals kept under intensive systems. Tudge [203] points out that they may be besieged and almost eaten alive by blowfly maggots in summer and die of cold and starvation in winter.

Where animals can express a choice between captivity and the wild, they do not always prefer the wild. In 1964, a group of African buffalo was captured in one region of Kenya for release in a National Park in another part of the country. While they were in captivity, they were kept in paddocks and fed regularly. When the time came for them to be set free, they frequently returned to the paddocks and it was very difficult to get rid of them (Thorpe [195]). Durrell [49] reported similar difficulties with animals he had captured to take back to zoos. Once, a revolution in Paraguay prevented him from taking the animals he had caught out of the country and they had to be released. Most of the animals had been in captivity for about 3 months and they simply refused to leave his camp at all, some of the parrots eating their way through wood and wire to get back into their cages.

These examples do not constitute an argument that all animals prefer the comforts of captivity to the hazards of the wild. But some may, and we cannot assume that animals will inevitably prefer their natural way of life over all others. Nor, as we have seen, can we assume that wild animals necessarily suffer less than captive ones. There is too much suffering in wild animals for a comparison between them and captive ones to be used as a standard for welfare unless there is a great deal of other supporting evidence.

We can now draw this chapter on 'natural' behaviour and its relation to suffering to a conclusion. For three separate reasons — the possible differences between domestic and wild animals, the lack of evidence about the effects of not performing certain behaviour patterns and the possibly unpleasant character of life in the wild — studies of presumed wild ancestors have limited value. They are unconvincing as a standard for welfare on their own. They do, however, have an extremely important function in assessing animal suffering and this is to tell us what the effects of captivity are and, through this, to alert us to the possibility that suffering is being caused. They can be used as a kind of warning system: 'Here is an area which needs looking at'. The restricted locomotion of animals, particularly very active ones, in small cages, would be an example of this. But, even studies which showed up major discrepancies between wild and confined animals would be a starting point only. For evidence that the differences were actually causing the animals to suffer, we have to look elsewhere.

5 *The physiology of suffering*

So far, we have seen that physical health is a valuable guide to an animal's well-being but that differences between wild and domestic animals do not in themselves provide an adequate criterion of suffering. There have, however, been hints of 'other evidence' that might be used to show more definitely whether an animal is suffering or not. In this chapter we will look at one source of that other evidence: the physiological state of the animal. The first problem here is to decide what to measure, that is, which physiological variables give the best indications of suffering.

As we shall see, physiologists have most commonly dealt with this problem using the concept of 'stress'. It might be thought that 'stress' and 'suffering' were one and the same thing. But it will become apparent that there are important differences between them. 'Suffering', as it has been used throughout this book, refers to a wide range of intense and unpleasant subjective states of people or other animals, such as fear and frustration. 'Stress' on the other hand, usually refers to a series of physiological changes, such as release of hormones, which go on within the body when an animal is subjected to injury, extremes of temperature, and so on. Under some circumstances, physiological changes which are called 'stress' may accompany subjective states of 'suffering'. But not always. And to make matters even more confusing, not everybody uses the word 'stress' in the same way. We will look at some of the different meanings of the word and at what physiologists have been able to measure in practice. But we must begin this chapter by looking at the physiological reactions that occur in animals that are physically harmed or in danger, for it is these that will enable us to understand where the idea of 'stress' comes from, and what its relation to 'suffering' might be.

The measurement of 'stress'

When an animal is suddenly faced with a situation in which it has to take some sort of rapid action such as running away or putting up a fight, its body changes in certain ways to meet the emergency. It breathes deeply to take in extra oxygen. The heart beats faster so that oxygen can be pumped more quickly to the tissues that need it. The liver releases sugar to fuel the muscles that will be used for fighting or running. This all happens very quickly, in a matter of a few minutes or seconds and Cannon [22] called it the 'General Emergency Reaction'. It is due to the activation of a special part of the nervous system, the sympathetic nervous system and of hormones such as adrenaline and noradrenaline. Very often, under natural conditions, when the animal's emergency resources are mobilized, it flees or fights off the source of danger and can then resume its normal and more peaceful activities.

It may happen, however, that these measures do not result in the source of danger being removed. If the animal is confined in a small cage, for example, so that it cannot flee from the attacks of other animals, the General Emergency Reaction will be continuously aroused, but to no avail. Then, its body begins to react in a rather different way. A new set of hormones are secreted. The most characteristic of these is ACTH (adreno-cortico-trophic-hormone) which is secreted by the pituitary gland at the base of the brain. The presence of ACTH in the blood is therefore a good indication that this second stage, sometimes known as the 'resistance' stage in the organism's response to danger, has begun.

ACTH stimulates the adrenal glands to produce a number of hormones, such as cortisone and hydrocortisone. These, in turn, help to keep the body provided with energy in the form of sugar. In this sense, the body's response is adaptive, maintaining the animal in a state of readiness to combat the source of harm.

Eventually, if the danger continues, the animal enters the final or 'exhaustion' stage of its response and its adaptive mechanisms start to break down altogether. The activity of various glands, such as the thyroid, begins to decline, growth in young animals slows down and sexual activity ceases. In males, fewer sperm are produced. In female mammals, embryos may be spontaneously aborted or, if the young are born, the mother may have no milk. Female birds lay fewer eggs. The blood itself changes in subtle ways, gastric ulcers may appear and the organism may become unable to resist infection. In fact, most of the organs of the body change in some way, usually to degenerate. But the overworked adrenal glands, still producing hormones, become bigger and bigger.

Selye [176] called this whole sequence, from the initial emergency responses to the stage of resistance right through to the exhaustion phase the General Adaptation Syndrome or GAS, to emphasize three aspects of it. He called it a syndrome because it affected so many different organs of the body. He called it an adaptation because, at least during the first stages, the response of the body was to help it to adapt to new conditions. And he called it general, because he believed that the general pattern of responses was the same whatever the precise nature of the danger, that is, whether the organism had been subjected to extreme cold, or injury, or starvation, or whatever.

In fact, it is now known that the body's response does vary depending on the kind of danger that it is exposed to. Extremes of heat and cold, for example, give rise to different physiological responses to those produced by the continued presence of aggressive members of the same species (Mason [137]; von Holst [85]). Nevertheless, Selye's original concept of a General Adaptation Syndrome or an all-purpose 'stress' response by the body has had a major impact on ideas about the physiological assessment of welfare. The rationale is as follows. Selye had described the way an animal's body responds to factors which are known to produce physical damage, such as starvation. Physical damage is, as we saw in Chapter 3, very likely to denote suffering. So, by measuring the 'stress' symptoms which accompany or precede overt injury or degeneration, the physiologist can be reasonably sure that he is measuring the symptoms which accompany or precede suffering. The fact that the body reacts in at least some of the same ways to a wide range of situations, only some of which cause overt damage, means that 'suffering' might now be recognized even when no physical injury is apparent.

For example, many animals including rats, voles and mice show some 'stress' symptoms when they are crowded together in a small space. In particular, they show enlarged adrenal glands typical of the second, resistance, stage of the General Adaptation Syndrome (Archer [1]). This has suggested that overcrowding causes these animals to suffer, even when they appear to be physically healthy. Similarly, it has been suggested that various forms of transport cause animals to suffer because they cause signs of hormonal and other disturbances characteristic of the GAS (Hails [72]).

The GAS is thus seen as an indicator that 'suffering', as recognized primarily through physical damage, is occurring, or that it would occur if the animal remained in those conditions for much longer. In other words, because of their association with physical injury and ill-health in some cases, 'stress' symptoms are used as labels for 'suffering' in others.

Using this idea, various kinds of measurements have been made, depending on the phase of the GAS that is being looked at. During the initial emergency reaction, changes in heart rate and in the levels of adrenaline and noradrenaline in the blood are obvious signs to look for. As an example of this, Candland *et al.* [21] found that there were large increases in the heart rates of cockerels when they were confronted with other strange cockerels and also when they were handled by a human being. Duncan and Filshie [46] found an unexpected effect on the heart rate of hens that they had subjected to various intense visual and auditory stimuli. One strain of hens, which they had called 'flighty' because of their extreme behavioural reactions to these stimuli, showed a sudden increase in heart rate and then a quite rapid return to normal heart rate once the disturbance was over. But another strain, which they had labelled 'docile' because of its calm behaviour, showed a rapid heart rate for much longer. The behavioural and physiological measurements seemed, then, to be giving rather different pictures of the birds' reactions.

In the later parts of the GAS, hormones such as ACTH and cortisone can be looked for. Baldwin and Stephens [6], for example, chased pigs around a yard with an electric goad and found that this resulted in an increase in these hormones, as did exposing them to cold. Kilgour and de Langen [113] studied hormone levels in sheep which were being subjected to various routine procedures such as being put into a truck, dipped or chased by a dog. They found that all of these resulted in a rise in the level of cortisone-type hormones but that none of them had nearly as much effect as separating the sheep from the rest of the flock. Thus, shearing a sheep, when it is taken away from the other sheep led to higher hormone levels even than slaughtering it, when the animals are together.

If everyone used the term 'stress' in exactly the same way, we could now go on to discuss the value of these and similar measurements as indicators of whether animals are suffering mentally. But unfortunately, as was mentioned before, stress is a word that is used in very different ways by different people and we must first make a short diversion to emphasize this point.

Some peoples' definitions of stress are so broad that they bear little, if any, relationship to the physiological symptoms of the GAS described by Selye as stress. For example, Coffey [28] calls stress 'any adversive stimulus', and, as Wood-Gush *et al.* [210] point out, it is sometimes used as a blanket term for any drop in productivity of, say, laying hens for which no-one has yet found any plausible explanation, let alone established evidence of the GAS. Sometimes the

Animal suffering

external stimulus which causes the physiological stress such as cold or heat is referred to as stress, whereas at other times the word refers to the response of the organism to the stimulus. Other definitions are concerned with the subjective feelings which are thought to be aroused at the same time as the physiological reactions. This usage is particularly apparent in discussions of human responses to noise, pollution and the pressures of modern living. Unpleasant features of human existence are said to be stressful but the connection with physiological symptoms of stress is not always established.

Even amongst definitions of stress that are tied to the General Adaptation Syndrome, there is no universal agreement. Sometimes 'stress' is taken to be synonymous with the whole of the GAS, including the initial emergency reactions. Sometimes it excludes this first part and involves only the later stages of resistance and exhaustion. For instance, Fraser *et al.* [60] say that an animal can be said to be in a state of stress "if it is required to make abnormal or extreme adjustments in its physiology or behaviour in order to cope with adverse aspects of its environment and management". Hails [72] interprets this as including the states both of coping with extreme conditions as well as becoming exhausted and failing to do so.

At other times, it is only the later stage of the GAS, when the adaptive mechanisms have broken down and the animal can no longer cope with the environment, which is called stress. Archer [1], for example, defines stress as "the prolonged inability to remove the source of a potential danger, leading to activation of systems for coping with danger beyond their range of efficiency", clearly emphasizing those aspects of stress which involve breakdown of the adaptive mechanisms. As if semantic difficulties were not enough, there has also been a tendency recently to add to the list of symptoms said to be characteristic of the GAS. The additions include changes in the liver, spleen and in body temperature (Duncan and Filshie [46]).

As the basic purpose of this chapter is to evaluate the usefulness of physiological measurements in animal welfare, we need not become too involved in these controversies over the definition of stress. We could not, however, have ignored them altogether because of the importance of stress in the development of ideas about the physiological assessment of suffering. What is particularly unfortunate is that some of the confusions about definition have led to some dubious conclusions about what factors cause 'stress' (Ewbank [53]). For example, Draper and Lake [41] injected hens with adrenaline and found that the numbers of eggs they laid decreased over the next few days. They also found that there were changes in the amount of sex hormones in the blood. These findings have been widely quoted as showing that 'stress' symptoms (e.g. increase in adrenaline) cause a drop in egg production and, more dangerously, that if egg production drops, the hens must be stressed. However, as these authors are themselves fully aware, the fact that physiological stress may cause a fall in egg production does not mean that *all* falls in egg production are due to the fact that the birds are 'stressed'. A change in the lighting pattern or in diet could cause hens to lay fewer eggs with no necessary symptoms of the physiological stress syndrome whatsoever.

Having seen some of the confusions that exist about 'stress', let us now turn to the wider problems of using physiological symptoms, such as those involved in the General Adaptation Syndrome, to tell us whether animals with these symptoms are suffering or not.

'Stress' and 'suffering'

A very oversimplified view might be that the presence of physiological 'stress' symptoms shows that an animal is suffering and the absence of such symptoms shows that it is not. We will now see how misleading such a view is, for although extreme stress symptoms indicate suffering, less extreme ones may actually be beneficial to the animal's well-being.

Perhaps the term 'stress', as a label for a group of physiological changes, is responsible for the common assumption that all stress is bad. In everyday language, to say that somebody is under stress implies that they are in a situation that they would rather not be in. This implication is reinforced by the knowledge that too much stress can be damaging to health. We have already mentioned gastric ulcers as an example of one of the 'diseases of stress'. The death of many animals which occurs while they are being transported is also thought to be due to extreme stress symptoms. For example, many transport deaths in pigs are from acute dilation of the heart which Hails [72] suggests is the result of the increased blood flow that occurs during the early part of the GAS.

While acknowledging the damaging nature of great physiological stress, however, many people, for example Brown [20], Fraser *et al.* [60], Kiley-Worthington [111] and Selye [177] also point out that some lesser stress symptoms may be a sign that an animal's body is coping with its environment. Far from being a sign of suffering, they may be an indication of well-being.

In support of this view, the physical health of animals which show some signs of the GAS can, in some cases, be shown to be better than that of animals which show no signs of it. For example, Marsh *et al.* [136] found that monkeys which had increased levels of corticosteroid hormones in their blood as a result of having to learn to press a lever to avoid shock were more resistant to poliomyelitis virus than unstressed monkeys. Similarly, mice which show some physiological stress have also been found to be more resistant to disease (Ferguson [56]).

This is not really all that surprising. As we saw earlier, the General Adaptation Syndrome is primarily an adaptive response by the animal's body, evolved to help it cope with emergencies such as disease. It has been found, for example, that the hormone ACTH, which is characteristic of the second or resistance stage of the GAS, appears to enhance an animal's ability to learn to avoid dangerous situations (Levine [127]). Rats with artificially reduced levels of ACTH were slower at learning to avoid electric shock than normal rats, but their ability to learn was restored to normal by giving them extra ACTH (Archer [1]).

An analogy might be drawn between the GAS and the central heating system of a house. The boiler is switched on whenever the temperature drops below a certain set-point, so that mere activation of the system does not mean that anything is amiss. Only if the temperature never reaches the set-point, or if the boiler overheats and bursts, do we conclude that the system is not working properly. Hence, by analogy, many classic signs of the early stages of the GAS may be an indication that the adaptive mechanisms are functioning.

Fraser *et al.* [60] have, therefore, suggested that well-being in an animal should not be taken as the complete absence of all signs of the General Adaptation Syndrome, but some kind of Happy Medium. This acknowledges the adaptive value of stress but still leaves the problem of deciding just what this Happy Medium should be for any given animal. At the present stage of research, we simply do not know how much of some physiological factor such as ACTH or adrenaline is desirable for an animal's physical well-being, let alone its mental well-being.

Similar problems arise in the interpretation of physiological measurements other than those classically described for the GAS, such as brain activity. Ruckebusch [166] recorded the electrical activity in the forebrains of horses, sheep, cattle and pigs and found characteristic patterns of change when the animals were moved to a new environment or given a different diet. He also found a pattern characteristic of week-ends when there was least interference from human beings. Ruckebusch suggests that brain activity, and particularly the time it takes for the activity to return to normal after a disturbance, could serve as an objective measure for ranking the severity of the disturbance from the animal's point of view. But here too there is the problem of translating a rank order into a measure of the amount of disturbance that is best for the well-being of the animal. Some stimulation may be positively desirable, as is shown by a study done by Duncan and Hughes [47]. They found that hens appeared to seek stimulation or 'interest' in their environment. They trained hens to obtain food by pecking at a disc on an automatic food dispenser. When the hens were given the choice between getting food by working for it in this way or by simply pecking at a pile of food in front of them, they chose to get at least part of their diet by operating the machine even though this was a slower way of getting food. We also saw in the last chapter that some animals seek stimulation to the extent of putting themselves in danger to obtain it.

In nature, animals are constantly bombarded by the stimulation of predators, aggressive individuals of their own species and so on. They have evolved both short-term and long-term physiological responses to deal with these situations. It would be wrong to assume that all stimulation and all 'stress' have to be avoided if animals are not to suffer. Too little as well as too much of either might cause suffering because, as Duncan [43] believes, animals may become bored. Physiological measures of suffering that we have available at the moment are not yet backed up with sufficient information for us to know where the Happy Medium lies.

A second reason why 'physiological stress' and subjective 'suffering' cannot, as yet, be directly related in all cases is that the relevant physiological measurements may not have been made. It is quite possible to believe that mental events are intimately tied up with and dependent upon physiological events and still to believe that the particular physiological variables that have so far been measured do not give an adequate picture of mental events. In other words, the emotional experiences which an animal has might depend on a great many factors besides the hormone concentrations in its blood and the weight of its adrenal glands. Even all available measurements put together might give only a very distorted and incomplete idea of the changes in mental state that are going on.

An experiment from the field of human psychology will illustrate this point. Even though this experiment involves asking human beings what they feel (a procedure that is, of course, denied us with any other species), it is nevertheless relevant to the problems of animal welfare because it acts as a cautionary tale. It shows that we must be very careful not to assume that the presence of a particular substance, adrenaline in the case we will discuss, always leads to similar subjective states under all circumstances.

Schachter and Singer [174] injected human volunteers with adrenaline and found that the subjective experiences which they reported depended on what they had been told the physiological effects would be and on what was going on around them. One group of volunteers was given a full description of the common effects of adrenaline such as increase in heart rate. Another group were given completely false information and told to expect itching and numbness, which are not known effects of adrenaline at all. A third group were not told anything, true or false, about what they would feel. In fact, none of the subjects realized the true purpose of the experiment. They all thought they were there to have their vision tested.

While the subjects were under the impression that they were just waiting for their turn to be tested, the real experiment had already begun. A stooge, pretending to be another subject, came into the room where a subject was waiting and went into one of two routines. He either acted in a 'euphoric' manner, throwing things around, making paper aeroplanes, etc., or he appeared to become extremely angry and eventually stormed out of the room. The experimenters watched the behaviour of the real subjects through a one-way mirror and also asked them to fill in a questionnaire about how they were feeling. They found that subjects who had been told correctly what the effects of their injection were likely to be tended not to take on the mood of the stooge. But subjects who had been misinformed or left in ignorance about the symptoms tended to become euphoric or angry depending on the behaviour of the stooge. Their reports of what they were subjectively feeling were influenced both by their expectations and what was going on around them. As

Schachter [173] emphasizes, there is no simple relationship between the hormone and the subsequent emotional state.

Brady [16], in a study on monkeys, also concludes that emotions are impossible to tie down to simple physiological variables. Von Holst [85] points out that hormones interact with one another, sometimes adding to each other's effects, sometimes cancelling out, so that reliance on the activity of just one hormone is almost certain to give misleading impressions of what an animal is experiencing.

Physiological measurements of suffering may one day give us a very good indication of the emotional states of animals. But, at the moment, the complexity of the factors which give rise to different emotional states is a major limitation on their use in the assessment of welfare. In addition, there are still some practical difficulties. One of these is that physiological measurements involve capturing and even damaging the animal in order to obtain them (Kiley-Worthington [111]; Murphy [151]). For example, adrenal glands can only be weighed when the animal is dead. Taking blood pressure or extracting blood to analyse the hormone content involves having leads attached to the animal and these, as Duncan [43] points out, may cause some suffering in their own right. So may having electrodes implanted in the brain to measure electrical activity. Recently, some of these problems have been overcome through the use of minute radio transmitters which, once they have been fixed onto or into the animal, cause minimal interference and can be used to monitor a wide range of variables such as temperature, heart rate and so on (Duncan [43]; Duncan and Filshie [46]). However, in general, physiological measurements do have the drawback of being a potential source of suffering before any measurements have even been made and in this respect they are less satisfactory as a method for assessing welfare than, say, observations of behaviour.

Another difficulty in practice is the variability of the physiological stress reaction itself. The General Adaptation Syndrome and 'stress' have been discussed so far as if the same reaction always occurred in an identical form in all animals.

However, this is very far from the practical experience of those who take the measurements. There may be considerable variation in the same individual at different times, for example. Baldwin and Stephens [6] observed very significant changes in the levels of hormones in pigs purely as a function of the time of day when they took the measurements. Animals from different strains or of different sexes may also differ (Murphy [151]). Pigs differ from other mammals such as monkeys (Baldwin and Stephens [6]) and even more from birds. Howard [89] found that injecting hens with adrenaline tended to decrease their heart rate, rather than to increase it as would be expected in a mammal.

In conclusion, we have seen that physiology holds out great promise for the assessment of suffering in animals because it can tell us what is going on beneath the skin, perhaps before any overt signs of ill-health are apparent. Physiological measurements such as those of heart rate or hormone levels can give an hour-to-hour or even moment-to-moment indication of changes in an animal's responses which would be hidden from the unaided observer. Potentially, they could be used to keep a particularly close watch on the state of the animal. At the moment, though, physiological measurements have a number of practical disadvantages such as that they interfere with the animal. They also have two serious conceptual problems. These are, first, what should be measured and, second, how to relate what is measured to the degree of suffering experienced by the animal.

As we have discussed, the identification of the 'stress' syndrome of the GAS has gone some way to answering the problem of what to measure. But it has not supplied the complete answer, since emotional states are complex and may not necessarily correlate closely with the relatively simple physiological variables that have been measured so far. Nor has it answered the problem of calibrating suffering with physiological measurements. Some levels of 'stress' and stimulation seem to be compatible with, and even desirable for, an animal's welfare. But what levels of hormone or other physiological variables should be called 'suffering' is not known. In some ways, the term 'stress' itself has caused so much confusion and been used in so many different ways that it may have lessened the contribution that physiology might have made to the assessment of an animal's welfare.

6   *Behaviour and suffering*

We have already met the idea that an animal's behaviour might be used to assess its welfare. In Chapter 4, we saw that one particular use of behaviour in this context — comparing captive with wild animals — did not turn out to be particularly reliable. But might there not be other ways in which behaviour could be used to indicate when animals are suffering? Do animals perhaps have particular signs that they give when they are experiencing unpleasant emotions? If it were possible to find out what these were, we would then have a very valuable way of judging what animals are feeling, one that would need no special instruments and would not interfere with the animals in the way that physiological measurements do.

The problem, as with physiology, is knowing what to look for. How can we interpret the language by which animals express their subjective feelings? In this chapter, we will look at three somewhat different ways in which people have attempted to answer this question and then at the difficulties they have encountered. The first way we will discuss arises directly out of the physiological approach we were discussing in the last chapter. Animals which show evidence of the group of physiological symptoms known as the General Adaptation Syndrome or GAS are watched to see whether they show any peculiar behaviour patterns associated with their disturbed internal state. Such behaviour is then used as an indication of suffering.

Next, we will examine a second way which assumes that animals may suffer even when physiological disturbances have not been looked for. The suffering might arise, for example, because the animal was fearful or because it was prevented from doing an action that it was strongly motivated to do. By deliberately putting animals into fearful or frustrating situations (and what this means will be described later), the behavioural signs of fear and frustration in that species can be discovered, whether or not anyone has yet looked to see if there are physiological symptoms as well.

Thirdly, we will look at an approach that derives mainly from observations on captive animals, such as those in zoos, which show highly 'abnormal' behaviour including biting their own tails and feet down to the bone. Because such behaviour is clearly damaging to the animal, most people have no hesitation in saying that the animal must be suffering. But a great deal of confusion has been caused because a wide variety of other behaviour patterns, not necessarily giving rise to physical damage, have also been labelled as 'abnormal'. As we will see, this has meant that the relationship between 'abnormality' and 'suffering' is not always easy to establish.

There may be a great deal of overlap between these three approaches. For example, some of the 'abnormal' behaviour seen in zoo animals turns out, on further investigation, to be very similar to frustration deliberately staged in the laboratory and may in turn be accompanied by physiological symptoms of stress. The point is not that there are three separate categories of behaviour but that, historically, there have been at least these three separate ways of identifying the behavioural expression of suffering in animals and the connection between them is not always made clear. Consequently, we will look at each approach separately, although trying wherever possible to see how they link together. Having done this, it will then be apparent that each of them faces a similar problem of 'calibration', that is, of saying how much behaviour corresponds to how much suffering.

Behaviour and physiological 'stress'

As described in Chapter 5, an animal's body responds to

impending danger or actual injury by a series of characteristic physiological changes that equip it either to run away or to fight off the hazard. These changes involve hormones and the nervous system and, not surprisingly, they also involve behaviour. At the first sign of anything new or unexpected, for example, most animals turn towards the disturbance, a process given the rather grand title of the 'orienting response'. If what is new is also dangerous or painful, the animal will take steps to protect itself, at first by reflexes such as blinking and later by responses such as running away, threat or overt aggression. External signs such as perspiration, erection of hair, urination and defeacation occur at the same time as the internal physiological changes such as increased heart rate, raised levels of adrenaline, and so on.

If these initial responses fail to have the effect of removing the animal from danger, the behaviour changes at the same time as the animal is, physiologically, going through the resistance and exhaustion phases of the GAS. The precise way in which behaviour changes is very variable (Archer [1]), but it may include increased aggressiveness or even, in one study by Barnett [9], a complete shift in the daily routine of subordinate animals (in this case, rats) so that they fed and were active only when the dominant animals were safely asleep. The variability in the behaviour of animals which show physiological stress does not, however, mean that there are no connections between the physiological symptoms of the GAS and the behaviour which accompanies them. All it means is that the 'stress behaviour' has to be separately identified and documented for each species. In chickens, for instance, individuals with the largest adrenal glands were found by Bareham [7] to be doing the most of a particular action called 'head flicks'. But in other species completely different actions are diagnostic of underlying physiological events.

As with the physiological responses, the behaviour of animals which show stress symptoms is, at least in the early stages, helpful to the animals. Increased aggressiveness, for instance, may initially be advantageous. In nature many animals have been shown to gain food, mates or freedom from interference by fighting. Gill and Wolf [67] showed that the Golden-winged Sunbird shows an increase in aggression whenever the flowers that it feeds on yield enough food to make up for the energy the birds expend in fighting over them. The birds gain from having their own 'private' flowers and being aggressive to other birds that encroach on them. Similarly, fear, responses to novelty, and so on, are important and adaptive features of animals' lives. We will tackle the difficult question of deciding *how much* stress behaviour an animal must show before we say that it is suffering later in the chapter. First, we will look at the other methods which have been proposed for identifying the behaviour of suffering.

Behaviour without signs of physiological stress

A number of scientists have become interested in the idea that it is not necessary to look for physiological stress to find out whether an animal is suffering. They believe that behaviour itself can provide the evidence.

Their basic reasoning is this. They assume that extreme fear or frustration are fundamentally unpleasant and cause suffering to animals, particularly if they are prolonged. They then attempt to find out how animals express the emotions associated with these states by deliberately exposing them to frightening or frustrating situations and seeing what they do. For example, an animal which has been deprived of food for a long time and would normally eat voraciously out of a certain dish, might be 'frustrated' by having the dish of food covered with glass, so that it could see it but not eat it. The behaviour which, say, pigs show under such circumstances can be recorded. Then, it is possible to look for signs of those same behaviour patterns in, for instance, intensively housed pigs and, on this basis, decide whether they, too are frustrated.

This line of argument is so important to an understanding

of many studies undertaken specifically to assess the welfare of animals that it is worth looking into in some detail. Wood-Gush *et al.* [210] believe that animals may suffer either when they are physically prevented from carrying out a particular action (like the animal with the glass-covered food) or in a conflict between two incompatible actions. How can we recognize when an animal is in a conflict? As with frustration, this can be experimentally devised. For example, a hungry animal might normally approach a particular dish and feed from it. The same animal might flee from an aggressive member of its species or from a man-made stimulus such as a flashing light. To produce a conflict, the animal is presented with a dish of food, but one which has a flashing light or an aggressive animal beside it. The animal is thus known to have a tendency to perform two actions (approach and run away) but cannot do both at the same time. It can thus be said to be in a conflict.

A considerable amount is now known about the behaviour which animals show when they are frustrated or in conflict. One thing that may happen when animals are strongly motivated to perform a behaviour pattern but the usual stimuli are not present is that they may show what have been called 'vacuum' activities instead. For instance, Morris [148] describes a raccoon which was kept in a cage without a female and began mating with its food-dish as a substitute. Hens in battery cages will similarly go through the complete movements of dust-bathing even when they are kept on wire floors and there is no dust. They also show nest-building behaviour as though they were picking up non-existent straws.

When animals are in a conflict, a very common reaction is to alternate, running first towards and then away from the source of conflict (Hinde [83]). At other times, they show a puzzling type of behaviour which has been called 'displacement activity' (Kortlandt [118]; Tinbergen [199]). The reason that it is puzzling is that the animal performs actions which seem to have nothing to do with the conflict it is in. For example, Arctic Terns which are in a conflict between approaching their nest and escaping from a human being will start to preen themselves (van Iersel and Bol [99]); and junglefowl cocks which are in a conflict between attacking another cock and fleeing often peck at objects on the ground (Kruijt [119]).

Perhaps the strangest responses to conflict and frustration have been discovered by psychologists in the course of training animals to perform various tasks in the laboratory. Masserman [138] describes some examples of what have been called 'experimental neuroses' in cats. One of his experiments involved training cats to press a switch to obtain food. At first, he reported, the cats appeared to be very 'happy' with this arrangement. They ran into the laboratory and purred while they pushed the switches. But then Masserman subjected them to various frustrations such as switches which did not work. The cats responded by pushing down everything in sight, including saucers and other cats and they became extremely agitated. In another experiment, cats and dogs which had been trained to operate a switch for food were suddenly given a blast of air. They were then in a conflict between pressing the switch and avoiding it altogether. They would then pace up and down, and one dog would never approach his food until he had circled it three times to the left and bowed his head in front of it.

These, then, are some of the behaviour patterns which animals show when they are known to be in conflict or frustrated. The occurrence of similar behaviour in some zoo and farm animals has been used by many people including Wood-Gush *et al.* [210] and van Putten and Dammers [161] as evidence for suffering in these animals.

The difficulty with trying to evaluate this view is that, almost without our knowing it, two separate questions become fused in our minds. The first question is: are conflict and frustration examples of unnatural behaviour shown only by animals in captivity? And the second is: do they indicate suffering, even when they occur in wild animals? The danger is that we assume that captive animals are unusual in being in conflict or frustrated and that this shows that they are suffering. It is much more constructive to consider the two questions separately.

The first is by far the easier to answer. Conflict and frustration do occur in wild animals and, what is more, they seem to be positively helpful to survival and reproduction. For example, Clutton-Brock *et al.* [26] showed that during the rutting season, Red Deer stags spend a great deal of time in conflict between whether to attack each other or to flee. The stags roar at each other and walk up and down in parallel for long periods of time. Clutton-Brock *et al.* found that the more closely matched two stags are in size, the longer they continue in this state of conflict. They argue that during the conflict, the stags are assessing each other and judging the likely fighting ability of their opponents. This is beneficial to both stags since fighting is a highly dangerous activity in which they run a high risk of being injured.

Displacement activities, too, appear to have an important function in the lives of the animals that do them. The displacement ground pecking that Junglefowl cocks do in the middle of a fight, for instance, is not irrelevant to fighting at all. Feekes [55] and Kruijt [119] showed that pecking the ground appears to make a cock more aggressive and more likely to be the winner of a fight.

The point of these examples is to show that conflict is a widespread occurrence in animals and, more importantly, that conflict behaviour patterns may be adaptive, enabling an animal to cope with the conflict and often eventually to resolve it.

The second question, of whether conflict and frustration show that an animal is suffering, is much more difficult to answer. Even if animals are showing adaptive behaviour, they may still be suffering in the process. Conflict may be beneficial in the long run but still be unpleasant while it lasts, just as pain may be adaptive, but still painful.

On the one hand, there are many examples of conflict behaviour where it would be very difficult to argue that animals were suffering. Dogs often turn round several times before settling down to sleep. This is a completely unnecessary movement on a sitting-room carpet and is a 'vacuum activity', a response to non-existent long grass which is to be flattened. Dogs also frequently chase balls, probably a substitute for real prey of which they are deprived. Few people would argue that dogs suffer because they show vacuum activities and respond to substitute stimuli. Quite the opposite seems to be the case. Dogs provide themselves with stimulation and make up for a lack of suitable live prey.

On the other hand, however, while conflict and frustration do not always indicate suffering, they sometimes certainly seem to. We saw in the last chapter that the prolonged activation of physiological defence mechanisms eventually leads to pathological symptoms and even death. Similarly, the persistance of behaviour associated with conflict also suggests that adaptive mechanisms are being overworked. In nature, conflict and frustration certainly occur. But they tend not to be prolonged over days or weeks. If an animal is attacked by other members of its species, for example, it will usually flee. But in captivity this is often not possible, so that an animal may be constantly stimulated to flee, but never can.

Inexorably, we have arrived back at the same problem of trying to find the Happy Medium that we have met before. Not all fear, frustration or conflict indicates suffering. But prolonged or intense occurrences of these same states may indicate great suffering. Where is the dividing line? Once again, we will postpone discussion of possible answers to this question until after we have discussed the third and final approach to the relationship between mental state and behaviour.

'Abnormal behaviour'

We will now look at a very large and mixed category of behaviour that has been described as 'abnormal'. 'Abnormal' does not just mean unusual. Broadhurst [18] and Fox [58], amongst others, all take it to mean a persistent, undesirable action, shown by a minority of the population which is not due to any obvious damage to the nervous system and which is generalized, that is, not confined to the situation that originally elicited it. Fraser [61] adds to this definition that the behaviour should be maladaptive or damaging to the animal, whereas Meyer-Holzapfel [145] excludes this from her definition.

At first sight, it may not seem obvious how abnormal behaviour differs from the kinds we have already discussed. The simple answer is that it may not differ at all. The reason for making a distinction is not because we are now going on to discuss a whole new category of behaviour, but because different assumptions are made about the way in which mental state is related to behaviour. In particular, we have seen repeatedly that 'stress' and behaviour such as that associated with fear and conflict do not always indicate that an animal is suffering.

The moment a behaviour is labelled 'abnormal' however, it becomes almost impossible to separate its occurrence from the implication that the animal doing it must be suffering because 'abnormal' is such an emotionally loaded word. So it seems valuable to discuss 'abnormal' behaviour in a separate section, at the same time as recognizing that there may turn out to be considerable overlap with some of the behaviour, such as fear and conflict, which we have already discussed, particularly when these are intense and prolonged.

There is one sort of abnormal behaviour which almost everyone agrees is a sign of severe suffering, namely when it results in actual physical damage, or death. Morris [148] describes various examples of this in zoo animals, such as monkeys that bit themselves so hard that they screamed with pain and a sulphur-crested cockatoo that pulled out all its feathers except a single one on the top of its head. Other examples come from farm animals. Pigs that are kept under intensive systems, for example, sometimes develop the habit of biting each other's ears and tails (Colyer [31]). Once the habit has started, other pigs join in and the pig which has been molested may be so wounded that it dies. When chickens are kept in large deep litter houses, they may show a kind of mass hysteria (Hanson [74]), which results in the birds piling up on top of each other and suffocating.

By the basic criterion of physical health discussed in Chapter 3, many of these examples of abnormal behaviour are generally accepted as indicating suffering in the animals that are damaged (although it is more controversial whether the animals that inflict the damage on others are also suffering). Even when the damage that results is only slight, animals sometimes behave so strangely that most people have little doubt that they are also very disturbed mentally. For example, Scottish Terriers which have been reared in isolation, show a bizarre 'whirling behaviour' (Thompson *et al.* [193]). The dogs appear to go into a fit, running jerkily in a tight circle, snapping at their own tails and yelping at the same time, and Rhesus monkeys which have been reared in isolation typically crouch in a corner, rocking to and fro and biting their own tails and genitalia (Berkson [13]; Draper and Bernstein [42]).

Although most people agree that such extremes of abnormal behaviour do indicate suffering, it does not follow that *all* abnormal behaviour does. The reason for this is that an enormous range of phenomena seen in many different animals under a wide variety of conditions has all been called 'abnormal behaviour'. The term has even been applied to displacement activities and other behaviour which is part of the 'normal' repertoire of a species. 'Abnormal behaviour', then is very diverse. It is likely that the mental states of the animals showing it are equally diverse.

At one extreme, it has been argued that abnormal behaviour gives pleasure to the animals that do it. Morris [148], for example, describes how some zoo-kept chimpanzees develop the habit of throwing faeces at human visitors, often with great accuracy and skill. By the definition given earlier, this is certainly an abnormal behaviour, including being very undesirable from the human point of view. But Morris argues that the animals find it very rewarding to watch people retreating in alarm and disgust. He offers a similar explanation for spitting at visitors by chimpanzees and orang-utans and flicking water by elephants. He also describes how some male animals such as chimpanzees and lions extract even more stimulation from their audience. They wait until a crowd has collected outside their cage and then aim a high intensity jet of urine at them. Some even save up part of the urine and direct a second jet when the first lot of people have retreated to mop themselves up and the ones behind have come curiously forward. Morris believes that all these animals enjoy the effects of their actions, abnormal though they are.

Other kinds of abnormal behaviour may, however, signify completely different mental states. Polar bears, foxes and tigers, for example, often pace backwards and forwards in their cages in zoos, tracing out a fixed pathway. Sometimes the floor of the cage becomes worn away where the animal has persistantly gone round in a circle or a figure of eight. Hediger [77, 78] believes that such fixed movement patterns are a sure sign that the animal is distressed.

In yet other cases, the mental state of the animals is very difficult to determine. A sloth bear (*Melursus*) was reported by Hediger to regurgitate its food after every meal and then eat it again. It would do this up to a hundred times after one meal. He also describes masturbation and eating of faeces as further examples of the abnormal behaviour which can occur in zoo animals. (Incidentally, Hediger points out that abnormal behaviour is not confined to the animals in the cages. He encountered one man who kept urinating into the mouth of a moose and another who threw religious pamphlets into the snake pit, apparently to banish the sins of the reptiles.)

These examples show that 'abnormality' is in itself a poor guide to the likely subjective states of the animals. It is yet another of the very confusing terms, such as 'stress' which appears to tell us more than it in fact does about the mental states of animals. Indeed, where abnormal behaviour has been systematically investigated, there appears to be considerable diversity in the factors which give rise to it and, by implication, perhaps also to the subjective states which accompany it. This point is illustrated particularly well by a kind of abnormal behaviour knowns as 'stereotypy'.

Stereotypies are simply actions that are performed in the same way over and over again. The repeated running backwards and forwards of caged carnivores which we have already mentioned has been described as a stereotypy. So have the rhythmic rocking movements shown by monkeys that have been reared in isolation. But Berkson [13] points out that there are many different sorts of stereotypes. The stereotyped locomotion of wild-born monkeys put into a cage consists of active movements of the whole body, such as jumping up and down. The stereotyped rocking of monkeys which have been reared in isolation, however, are usually done by an animal sitting in one place without moving around. Both are stereotypes, both have been described as abnormal, but the movements look quite different and, Berkson, argues, they are caused by quite different factors.

Similarly, Keiper [107] has shown that an abnormal stereotyped action called 'spot-picking' which is seen in caged canaries, is related to the way the birds get their food. But another abnormal action, moving along a fixed pathway, appears to be a response to being in a small cage.

Relating behaviour to degree of suffering

We have now seen that each of the ways in which people have tried to make the connection between what an animal does and what it feels runs into difficulties. The behaviour associated with physiological 'stress' and with fear, conflict, frustration and so on are useful guides, but we cannot equate well-being with the complete absence of any of them.

'Abnormal' behaviour poses even more problems because it is such a wide term, although it may be possible to learn about the factors which give rise to such behaviour and thus come closer to learning about the subjective state of the animal. For example, abnormal 'pacing' in battery caged hens in the hour or so before they lay an egg has been shown by Wood-Gush [209] to be due to frustration at not having a nest in which to lay the egg. But this, too, runs into the same difficulty of knowing how much frustration can be said to constitute suffering.

There are two main ways in which people have attempted to come to terms with the problem of 'calibrating' the degree of suffering which an animal experiences with its behaviour. One way, which we can call the 'hard-line' criterion, is to say that no behaviour can be used as evidence that an animal is suffering unless it can be shown to involve physical ill-health or to be a precursor of it. Some farmers, for example, have reported that their pigs had been particularly active in the few days before an outbreak of tail-biting (Ewbank [52]). If it turned out to be possible to predict when such an outbreak was likely to occur because the animals were behaving in particular ways, then their behaviour might be used as signs that they were not in a state of well-being. Or, if it were shown that a certain degree of frustration led to physical symptoms of ill-health, this too might be used as evidence of suffering even before the health of the animals was demonstrably affected.

The intensity of frustration that is defined as showing suffering would thus be that which, if continued, would lead to physical damage, illness or death. This would involve relying mainly on physical health as a guide, but extending it backwards in time to include known precursors or danger signals. So, whether, say, stereotyped movement patterns in caged animals are taken as showing that the animals are suffering would be judged not by whether they were 'abnormal' or 'unusual' but by whether they could be shown to be the precursors of coming illness.

Many people feel, however, that the hard-line criterion is inadequate. They believe that animals suffer even when there is no evidence of physical ill-health, present or impending. They therefore have to decide how much frustration, for instance, an animal can show before it should be described as suffering. As this chapter has shown, it is possible to identify the behaviour patterns associated with numerous unpleasant emotional states such as fear and conflict. These terms can be objectively defined and situations set up in which it is possible to investigate their occurrence. But, as we have seen, not all instances of such behaviour patterns necessarily indicate suffering so that there are still considerable difficulties of 'calibration'.

Nevertheless, assessments of suffering do not have to be wild guesses. They may contain a subjective element, but they can at least be based on knowledge of the animals concerned. For example, it is possible to find out whether a particular animal, such as a sow in a rearing pen is frustrated or not. It is also possible to find out how long that frustration lasts and the factors that reduce or increase it. While such information does not, of course, *solve* the problem of calibrating behaviour with degree of distress, it at least provides a factual base on which to make decisions. The subjective assessments can be informed.

In conclusion to this chapter, we can refer to the Brambell Committee [17] which firmly stated that: "Animals show unmistakable signs of suffering from pain, exhaustion, fright, frustration and so forth and the better we are acquainted with them the more readily we can detect these signs". This is a hopeful view. But we have also seen that there are considerable problems over using behaviour in the assessment of welfare. The raw materials on which we have to work are either completely new behaviour patterns which are the result of captivity or more frequent or more intense versions of behaviour also seen in less restricted conditions. We have seen that it would be a mistake to regard any occurrence of abnormal or unusual behaviour as necessarily indicating that an animal is suffering. We have to find a Happy Medium. And that is still a problem.

7   *What animals choose*

If we want to try to understand the subjective feelings of animals, we have to try to see the world 'from the animals' point of view'. Obviously, non-human animals cannot tell us in so many words whether they are suffering. But, as we will see in this chapter, it may be possible to allow them to express at least some of their feelings, if not in words, then in actions. The particular actions which have been suggested for this role are those that result from what the animals *choose* and what they regard as *rewarding* and *punishing*. We will discuss both the advantages and the dangers of using this method as a way of assessing suffering. But first, we will see why it has been thought that choice, reward and punishment should be able to tell us anything at all about an animal's feelings.

Preference, welfare and suffering

A hundred years ago, Spencer [189] suggested that a connection might exist between the subjective feelings of animals, their choice of environment and their welfare in that environment. He argued that subjective feelings such as pleasure and pain might have evolved to help animals to seek out conditions which were best for their survival and avoid conditions which were harmful to them. He saw disagreeable feelings of pain or other kinds of suffering as a sort of internal stimulus, causing the animal to move away and find some other environment. Animals that experienced suffering when they found themselves in conditions which were harmful to their well-being and took steps to find somewhere else, he said, would survive better than those that derived pleasure from the harmful environment and stayed in it.

Spencer's idea of a possible link between the subjective feelings of animals on the one hand and environments likely to benefit or harm them on the other has been taken up by many biologists since. Lack [124], for example, explained the fact that different bird species live in different habitats by saying that birds 'like' particular areas to live in. He suggested that birds would fly over a certain area and then decide to settle down or move on depending on what they found there. Particular sorts of trees, nesting holes or shade might be some of the things that affected their choice of a home. Lack also believed that the environment which most attracted a bird would be the one that would be best for its chances of surviving and rearing young. Orians [153] similarly argued that birds should be, as he put it, more 'turned on' by places in which their survival chances are best.

Field studies have subsequently shown that many animals have definite preferences about where they choose to live and, in addition, that the environments which they prefer do also seem to be the ones in which they are most successful (Hildén [82]; Klopfer and Hailman [114]; Partridge [155]). An example of this is the Peppered moth, which chooses to rest in places which give it the best protection from being eaten by birds. This moth comes in two colours. The pale, off-white version is best camouflaged when it is sitting on a tree-trunk covered with lichen. The darker, sooty version is best hidden on dark tree trunks with no lichen such as occur in areas polluted by industrial smoke. Birds are more likely to eat moths sitting on the wrong sort of tree-trunk (Kettlewell [109]) and the moths themselves are most likely to settle on the sort of tree-trunk they most resemble (Kettlewell and Conn [110]).

Experimental psychologists, too, have been influenced by Spencer's ideas particularly in the study of the way in which animals learn (Bolles [14]). And it is here, in the psychologist's laboratory, that we find the key to being able to ask an animal how it feels and find the answer in what it does.

Psychologists very frequently train animals to make some kind of response, such as pushing a lever if the animal is a rat, pecking a key if it is a pigeon or swimming through a loop if it is a goldfish. Every time the animal does what is required, it is rewarded in some way, often by being given a bit of food. The food is referred to as a 'positive reinforcer' because it makes the animal more likely to make the same response again. There are other stimuli, however, that are known as 'negative reinforcers' or punishments which make the animal less likely to make the same response again. An electric shock is an example of a negative reinforcer. Not surprisingly, a rat will not keep pressing a lever if every time it does so it gets an electric shock through its feet. In fact, it will learn quite complicated tasks solely in order to avoid getting a shock.

Positive and negative reinforcers are a window on animal feelings. Psychologists use them to present their animals with a series of choices, such as whether to continue to press a lever or not. The animals then have to make an informed choice, informed, that is, because they have learnt the consequences of each course of action (pressing the lever or not) from previous experience. What is of interest is whether the animal responds to the situation by trying to repeat the consequences of its actions or by trying to avoid them. It is this that tells us what the animal may be experiencing subjectively when it receives the reinforcement.

By making the simple assumption that animals experience subjective feelings of pleasure in the presence of rewards or positive reinforcers and that they experience distress in the presence of punishments or negative reinforcers, it has been suggested that such training techniques could provide an objective way of finding out what animals are feeling. The advantage of this approach is that no assumptions about what is rewarding or punishing have to be made beforehand. This can be discovered in each case from how the animal responds. And what is particularly important for the study of welfare is that it is not just food and shock which can act as reinforcers, but a wide range of other situations as well. It is thus possible to find out the animal's 'view' of many different objects and environments. For example, hamsters will learn to press a lever simply to get strips of paper. They then tear this up for nest material (Jansen *et al* [102]). Mice keep pressing a lever for paper even when they have completed their nests. They seem to find gathering up nest material reinforcing in itself (Roper [165]). Chaffinches will learn to sit on a particular perch just to hear a tape-recording of another chaffinch (Stevenson [192]). And male Siamese Fighting fish find it rewarding to be able to see another male fish so that they can display aggressively at it (Thompson [194]). But perhaps the most unusual reinforcer of all has been found by Losey and Margules [130] in the Butterfly fish (*Chaetodon*). This is a marine fish which lives in the sea near Hawaii. It can be rewarded by a very crude model of a fish which, in nature, removes parasites from its skin by eating them. The real parasite-removing fish is a wrasse (*Labroides*) which, because of its role in life, is known as a cleaner fish. When the Butterfly fish sees a model of its cleaner (which does not, of course, remove any parasites from it), it rubs up against it and shows a special 'invitation to be cleaned' posture that it would show to a real fish. Losey and Margules kept butterfly fish in a tank and showed that they would learn to go to a particular place to be shown the model cleaner. Then, when the model was removed, they operated the apparatus to get the model back again. So, clearly, training techniques have a very broad application.

Russell and Burch [168] were among the first to recognize the possibilities this might have for the assessment of animal welfare. They argued that one of the best criteria for deciding whether a given set of conditions caused an animal to suffer was whether those conditions could be shown to act as negative reinforcement. Their basis for saying this was the close link they believed existed between what causes suffering and what the animal regards as punishment. On their view, animals would learn to avoid situations in which they suffered and in turn suffering could be recognized by whether the animals learnt to avoid them.

Recently, Jürgens [105] has applied this criterion to

Squirrel monkeys. The monkeys easily learnt to press switches to obtain food. The calls they gave while they were doing this he called pleasure calls. But other calls they only gave when they were pressing switches to avoid or terminate something. These calls, because they were given in the presence of negative reinforcers, he believed showed that the monkeys were distressed.

We can now see that there are two threads, both leading back to Spencer, that connect choice or learning with animal welfare. One is the idea that subjective feelings of pleasure, pain and suffering are related to an animal's chances of health and survival in different environments. The other is that these subjective feelings result in the animal doing certain things, such as learning to avoid or repeat certain actions. Studying what the animal does, and in particular what it demonstrates to us as being positive and negative reinforcers, is therefore seen as a way of finding out about the subjective feelings and also about the animals welfare in different environments. As we will see by the end of this chapter, both of these threads have their flaws. The connections between reinforcement, subjective feelings and welfare are not always that straightforward. But they are a beginning. We can effectively ask an animal how it regards a particular environment. Is it something attractive, to be approached at first and then worked for in an attempt to repeat the experience of gaining access to it? Or is it something to be avoided?

The important thing about such questions is that they are an objective way of trying to find out how the animal views its environment. They are animal-centred, not human-centred questions. We will now look at some of the answers which animals have given.

Choice tests in animal welfare

A number of experiments have now been done to find out what sorts of environments animals choose when they are given the opportunity and the sorts of situations that they find positively and negatively reinforcing. One of the most informative of these was a study done by Hughes and Black [93] on battery-kept hens. It had been strongly recommended by the Brambell Committee [17] that the floors of battery cages should not be made of fine-gauge hexagonal wire. The Committee thought that this was uncomfortable for the hens to stand on. They recommended instead that the floors of all cages should be made of heavy rectangular metal mesh. If this 'Brambell' floor had been widely adopted, it would have been extremely expensive because it had a tendency to cause eggs to crack. What was more serious from the welfare point of view was that there was no evidence that hens found it more comfortable to stand on.

When the hens were given the opportunity to choose for themselves between different sorts of floors, their verdict was very different from that of the Brambell Committee. Hughes and Black measured their preference by the amount of time they chose to stand on a particular type of floor. The hens clearly preferred to stand on the fine-gauge wire condemned as uncomfortable by the Committee instead of on the coarser type which they had recommended. Photographs taken from below of the hens standing on different sorts of floors showed that their feet were more supported by the finer mesh.

Concern for hens in battery cages does not stop, of course, with finding out which sort of floor they prefer to stand on. Many people would feel that this was only finding out which the hens saw as the lesser of two evils. More extensive preference tests have therefore been done to find out how hens view the whole environment of a battery cage. In one series of experiments, hens were offered a choice between a battery cage and an outside run in the garden (Dawkins [37, 38]). This choice was presented to them in the form of a choice corridor. By looking in one direction, the hen saw one environment and by looking in the opposite direction, it saw the other one. The hen was free to walk into either one. It is obviously somewhat difficult logistically to move a whole battery hen-house around, so the battery cage in the choice test was housed in a small hut on wheels, lit and heated as much as possible like a battery house but with the advantage that it was manoeverable. It could therefore be made to appear either on the hen's left or its right, making it possible to control for any positional biasses the hen might have.

For the actual test, the hens were given free access to both environments, allowed to make their choice and then confined for 5 min in whichever one they chose. After this they were given the same choice over again, for a total of 24 separate choices and confinements for each individual hen. Each bird thus accumulated experience of the environments which it chose and it was possible to see whether it showed an increased or decreased tendency to enter each one. In other words, it was a way of finding out whether the battery cage and the outside run were acting as positive or negative reinforcers.

As might be expected, the hens had an overall tendency to choose the outside run, although their choices were quite strongly influenced by the sorts of conditions they had been living in before the test began. Hens which had been living in an outside run all chose the outside run right from the very first choice. Hens which had previously been living in battery cages, on the other hand, tended to choose very differently, at least at first. They initially tended to choose the battery cage. However, the more experience they had of the run, the more likely they were to choose it when they next had the choice. A few minutes' experience of being in an outside run seemed enough to make them, too, prefer the run, which appeared therefore to be a positive reinforcement.

Now the obvious rejoinder to the finding that hens prefer being outside in a run to being inside in a battery cage is that this does not tell us anything about whether they suffer in battery cages. A gourmet might prefer caviare to smoked salmon, but it would be difficult to argue that he would suffer if he had to make do with smoked salmon. This is another way of saying that preference by itself is not an indicator of suffering. To show that a preference does indicate suffering in the less preferred environment, we have to find out not merely what the preference is, but how strong it is. If it were shown that hens would do literally anything to get out of a battery cage and that their preference for the run was so strong that it overruled everything else, then it might be possible to conclude that they suffered in cages. If, on the other hand, the preference for the run did not seem to be very strong, such a conclusion would seem much less justified.

A lot hinges, then, on being able to measure the strength of the preference for one environment over the other. So far, attempts to do this have yielded unsatisfactory results. In one experiment, the strength of the preference was measured by seeing whether the hens were willing to forgo food in order to get into the run. Food was thus used as a kind of yardstick against which to measure preference. When hens which had been living outside were offered a choice between an outside run with no food and a battery cage with food, they all unhesitatingly chose the run (Dawkins, in prep.). Battery-caged hens given the same choice, however, were less decisive and some of them chose the cage. Birds, even those used to outside conditions, which had been made slightly hungry tended to go wherever food was to be found even though this meant having to go into a cage to get it.

But while it is difficult to measure strength of preference, it is, in principle, possible to do so, along the lines we have discussed. It is also possible to 'dissect' a battery cage to find out which aspects of it a hen finds attractive or aversive. The information gained from this type of experiment could be very important when legislation is formulated. We have already seen how the well-meaning recommendation of the Brambell Committee about cage floors was not endorsed by the hens themselves. A number of alternatives to conventional battery cages have been designed (e.g. Bareham [8]). Choice tests might be one way of finding out whether the animals regarded them as significant improvements.

Although the choices of chickens have been more extensively studied in relation to welfare problems than those of most other animals, the method can also be applied to any animal. Pigs, for instance, are very good at operating machinery. Baldwin and Meese [5] trained pigs to work various devices with their snouts to find out what pattern of light and darkness they preferred. The amount of light that pigs should have is controversial. Commercially, some pigs are kept in almost continual semi-darkness to try to reduce the incidence of behaviour such as tail-biting which was mentioned in the last chapter. Many people object to this practice, but it might be possible to ask the pigs for their views.

Baldwin and Meese gave their pigs a simple method for turning lights on and off for themselves which was to break an infra-red beam with their snouts. The pigs showed a definite preference for light over darkness and they gave themselves some light even at night. Baldwin and Meese suggest that similar tests on the preferred intensity of light would be an objective way of resolving the controversies about the amount of light that pigs should have.

In another series of experiments by Baldwin and Ingram [4], pigs showed that they could easily learn to regulate the temperature of their environment. Pigs which were kept in a cold room ($-5°$ C) quickly learnt to push a switch that turned on a heater for 3 s. One pig took only 5 min to realize the connection between the switch and the heat and began to switch on the heater with no previous training at all.

Choice tests and learning experiments could be a very valuable way of finding out how animals view their environments. We have only just begun to exploit the full potential of these methods. One day they might be used to establish objective standards of welfare based on what the animals are known to find attractive or aversive (Baldwin and Meese [5]; Dawkins [37, 38]; Hughes [91]; Kilgour [112]; Murphy [151]). Animals may not be able to talk, but they can vote with their feet and express some of what they are feeling by where they choose to go. If they were to be provided with the right electronic gadgetry, who knows what they could tell us, by voting with their snouts or their paws or their beaks?

Objections to choice tests

Despite their obvious attraction, there are a number of serious objections to choice tests as a tool in the assessment of animal welfare. As we will now see, they do not provide all the answers to problems about the physical and mental well-being of animals.

In the first place, as Duncan [44, 45] points out, an animal's short-term preferences may not be the same as what it would choose in the long run. He gives the example of hens which choose to enter trap-nests to lay their eggs. The result of going into a trap-nest is that a hen is then confined in it for several hours without food, water or social contact. At the time of laying, the preference for the nest is so strong that it overrides these subsequent effects. Day after day the hens will choose to go into the nests and then be deprived for several hours afterwards. A hen which was deprived of food and water and then tested at some time other than when she was about to lay an egg would probably choose food and water in preference to a nest. But a hen which has already chosen a nest is forced to 'make do' without them for the rest of the day.

This is by no means an isolated example. Many animals behave differently at different times of the year, different stages of their breeding cycle and so on. Their preferences for different environments, too, may vary. So we have to be careful not to conclude too much from a single preference test. It does not mean, however, that the whole idea of using an animal's choices to assess its welfare has to be abandoned because it is possible to find out whether short-term and long-term preferences are different. An experiment could be done to find out whether hens do, in fact, choose differently at different times of the day and ideas about the hens 'preferred' environment could then be adjusted accordingly.

The choice tests which have been done so far could be criticised on the grounds that the possible discrepancies between short-term and long-term preferences have not been adequately explored. But the general idea of using choice tests cannot be criticised on these grounds, because the criticism could be answered if enough information were available. The principle remains valid.

Much the same can be said of another objection which has been levelled at choice tests — that what animals apparently prefer varies with the method of testing, with the breed of animal and even with the individual animal and so on. It is certainly true that what an animal chooses does depend on many such factors. Hughes [91], for example, demonstrated clearly that the floor preferences of hens could appear to be different depending on the way he carried out the test. When he measured their preference by counting how much time the birds spent standing on wire or on a litter floor and gave them the freedom to move between the two, he found no overall preference for one floor or the other. But when he measured preference in a repeated two-choice situation and confined the bird for several hours in a cage with whichever floor it chose after each choice, most of the hens preferred the litter.

The fact that animals may choose differently under different circumstances is a major difficulty in interpreting their preferences for welfare purposes. But it is a problem that is in no way unique to choice tests. We have seen repeatedly throughout this book that animals vary. They vary from species to species and from individual to individual. They also vary in their physiological responses, and in behaviour, and both genetic and environmental factors contribute to this variability, making it very difficult to make generalized statements about animal suffering, whichever criterion is being used. That does not mean, however, that we have to give up the search for general conclusions altogether. Instead, we should do the relevant experiments to find out what factors are important.

The experiment by Hughes [91], which was just mentioned, is a good example of how this can be done. Hughes did, in fact, use two strains of hens, to see whether their preferences differed. He also designed the experiment to see whether the previous experience that the birds had had made a difference to what they chose. So some of his birds had experience of litter and others of wire floors. By using the powerful statistical technique known as the Analysis of Variance, he was able to obtain a quantitative estimate of the importance of each factor. Thus, he found that for one of his methods of testing, the birds' previous experience was a significant factor in what they chose, but the strain of the bird and the time of day at which the tests were carried out were not.

In other words, the possibility that many different factors can all influence the way an animal behaves, including what it apparently prefers, is not a reason for abandoning the study of its choices altogether. Many things do affect preferences — we cannot escape from that. But what we can do is systematically to investigate the way these factors operate and whether or not they are important. Some preferences might turn out to be fairly robust, in that they are shown by all members of a species, however they are tested and whenever the tests are carried out. Other preferences might turn out not to be so universal, but the variation itself might be instructive. For example, we have seen that the environmental preferences of hens can be affected by where they have been living (Dawkins [37, 38]). This in itself suggests that the battery-cage system should be evaluated separately for birds which have been reared on deep litter and those that have been in cages all their lives.

It is an important criticism of choice tests in welfare that many factors influence choice. It is, however, a criticism that the right experiments have not yet been done. It shows again that more work needs to be done, not that the idea is wrong.

We must now tackle what is probably the most serious single objection to the use of preference tests, namely, that animals do not always choose what is best for their own long-term physical well-being. We saw at the beginning of this chapter that many biologists believe, on evolutionary grounds, that there is probably some connection between what animals choose on the one hand and what is best for their survival and reproduction on the other. The connection is not, however, a hard and fast one. Animals do not always choose what is best for them.

Duncan [44, 45] again provides valuable examples. Domestic cattle do not always choose their food wisely.

Sometimes they eat poisonous plants or bloat themselves with clover. Animals such as pigs and rats have a strong liking for saccharine, and yet it has no food value. We can add other examples from everyday experience: people choose to smoke and do other things which may damage their health in the long run.

Duncan argues that, in animals, breakdowns in the 'wisdom of the body' are the result of domestication. He believes that natural choice mechanisms have been distorted by artificial selection and that human beings often prevent young animals from learning from their parents. While this may be true, domestication is not the only reason why animals do not always choose wisely. Wild animals, too, make mistakes.

Tinbergen [198] gives a dramatic example. He found that an Oystercatcher preferred to incubate an egg much larger than its own. If given the choice, it would try to sit on an ostrich-sized egg, leaving its own unattended. Baerends and Kruijt [2] showed that Herring Gulls also chose eggs which were much larger than their own. The larger the eggs were, the more likely the birds were to choose them. A large egg acts as a 'supernormal' stimulus.

The explanation for this aberrant preference is that the birds are being put into an artificial situation. Normally, ostrich eggs do not appear in the nests of English gulls, so a bird which responds to the largest egg-like objects in sight will end up incubating its own eggs. It will only make a mistake when an interfering ethologist deliberately makes 'own egg' and 'largest egg around' no longer the same thing.

The fact that many animals have such a liking for non-nutritive saccharine can probably be explained in a similar way. In nature, a sweet taste almost always denotes food. Only when the taste and the nutritional value are artificially separated are the animals 'fooled'.

This idea can be expressed more generally. Many biologists have emphasized that a distinction should be drawn between the evolutionary reasons for a behaviour (known as its survival value or adaptive significance) and the stimuli to which the animal responds in its everyday life. This is a particularly important distinction to maintain when talking about preference. The evolutionary advantage that a bird gains, for example, from defending a territory might be that it secures for itself a private food supply. But the bird might not have any direct way of measuring how much food there was in a particular area. Even if a bird chooses to set up a territory where there is a lot of food, this would not necessarily show that the bird had counted the amount of food there. It might simply have chosen the territory on the basis of some other characteristic such as the number of trees. Now, provided there was a good correlation between the number of trees and the amount of food, this would be an easy way to select a good territory. It might be much easier for the bird to respond to trees than to make a direct count of the amount of food. So the ultimate evolutionary advantage (a large food supply) might be different from the proximate stimuli (trees) to which the bird actually responds. In this environment, a bird which had a preference for a territory with a lot of trees would effectively be expressing a preference for a territory with a good food supply, because the two go together. But in another environment, where trees were not a good indicator of food, the same bird might choose 'unwisely' if it responded to the same proximate stimulus.

In the artificial environments in which human beings frequently keep animals, the correlations that exist in nature have often disappeared. There are sweet substances that have no food value, for instance. The proximate and ultimate factors in an animal's choice may become separated. It may respond to a proximate stimulus which, ultimately, is harmful. Such a consideration applies both to wild animals and to domesticated ones. Add to this the effects of captivity and generations of selective breeding and there is an even greater possibility of a separation between what is chosen and what is beneficial.

So we can see that there are serious objections to using animal choices as a guide to their welfare. These objections mean that we should never use choice tests as the sole criterion of welfare. None of the methods which we have considered, however, are entirely satisfactory on their own. Each has its drawbacks and is best used in conjunction with the others as discussed in Chapter 9.

There are some cases, indeed, where the animal's preferences would be a positively misleading guide to their long-term health and well-being. If a dog were to be given the choice between going to the vet, and not going, it would probably choose not to go. The panic which is caused among some farm animals by the sight of someone in a white coat (Kiley-Worthington [111]) is an indication of their view of medical treatment. Nevertheless, we decide that animals should be treated by a vet, just as we drag protesting children to the dentist. Short-term preferences are in these cases overruled in favour of the known long-term advantages to physical health.

In the course of this chapter, we have seen that some of the difficulties with using choice tests to evaluate welfare relate to the problem of documenting what an animal's preferences are, and how they vary according to such factors as the method of testing, previous experience of the animal and so on. Other difficulties arise from the fact that animals do not always choose what is best for their physical health in the long run. Sometimes, of course, what animals choose will be compatible with conditions known to be beneficial to their welfare on other grounds. What they like might even give us clues as to how we might improve their physical health. But the objections to the use of choice tests for evaluating welfare should not, in any case, blind us to the very real advantages they also bring. For, properly used and taken in the context of information from other sources, they give us the closest approach we yet have to being able to ask an animal what it is feeling.

8   Analogies with ourselves

The final method for assessing animal suffering that we will look at is that of using ourselves as models of what animals might be feeling. Many people may believe that this should have been the first method to consider. But reserving it until after all the other methods have been discussed is deliberate. Our ideas about the mental experiences of other species have, ultimately, to come from some kind of analogy with ourselves, just as they do with other human beings (Brambell [17]). 'Ultimately', however, is the key word. The theme of this book is that, first, we must look at all the evidence we can about the animals concerned, particularly their behaviour, physiology and external appearance. We should learn as much as we can about their social behaviour, ways of expressing emotions such as fear, their powers of learning and memory and so on. None of these will supply the whole picture of what animals experience subjectively. There will come a time when information from all sources is put together (Chapter 9) and a human assessment is made of the feelings of other species. Such an assessment will inevitably rely on recognition of some similarity between ourselves and other species to make the final leap between what is observed directly by us and what is experienced subjectively by them. The important thing is that the final assessment is based on all the available evidence on the animals concerned and not just on well-meaning guesswork.

Although we cannot escape from analogies with ourselves to tell us about feelings in other animals, we can at least make sure that our analogies are as accurate as possible, that is, that we have taken into account both the similarities and the differences that exist between ourselves and other species. In this chapter, we will be trying to find the difficult path between two opposite pitfalls. To one side of this path lies the danger of thinking of other species as so different from human beings that there is no analogy to be drawn at all. To the other is that of thinking that the subjective feelings of other animals are identical to our own and that all we need to do to understand animals is to project our own feelings onto them (Thorpe [195]). We will discuss the drawbacks of using analogies with ourselves to assess animal suffering, beginning with a clarification of what is meant by such analogies.

Dangers of analogies with ourselves

There are two somewhat different ways in which people use their own feelings to make inferences about the feelings of other animals. The most direct way is to observe what an animal does and then to use similarities between its behaviour and their own as evidence for similarity in mental state. For example, if an injured animal cries and limps, we know we behave similarly when we are injured, and might infer that the animal experiences pain as we do. This is a version of what philosophers call the 'argument from analogy'. The second way is more indirect and is by far the most common in debates about animal welfare. It does not rely on watching or hearing an animal but on trying to imagine oneself in the situation of the animal. The question 'How would you like to live in a battery cage?' is an appeal to this kind of analogy. It can be used by someone who has never seen chickens kept commercially.

The conclusions that are drawn about an animal's state of mind can be quite different depending upon which kind of analogy is being used. If we sit at home and imagine what it might be like to be an animal in a particular situation, we might have one picture. But if we then went and looked at the animal, we might get a totally different impression. It is important to be aware of this distinction because the two sorts of analogy are liable to rather different sorts of error.

Analogies of the first sort carry with them the danger that people may misinterpret the gestures or sounds of the animals in front of them. For example, someone unfamiliar with the behaviour of a rat, hamster or other small rodent might interpret the 'freezing' posture, in which the animal crouches and remains still as showing that the animal is feeling restful or even sleepy. Studies of the sort described in Chapter 6, however, have shown that freezing is a symptom of fear and is the way these animals frequently respond to the appearance of a predator.

In many cases, misunderstandings that arise over the meaning of animal gestures can be cleared up by greater knowledge of the particular species, along the lines already discussed in the course of this book. There are over a million species of living animals and many of them have very different ways of expressing their feelings from the way that we do. Unless we take the trouble to study them we are very liable to misinterpret them.

Analogies of the second sort — trying to put ourselves in an animal's place — are even more dangerous. The dangers come not from attempting to imagine what the animal might be feeling, but from imagining the situation through human eyes and ignoring basic biological facts about the animal. How revolting, one might think from a human point of view, to be a bat, to live in a dark cave and have to eat live insects, legs and all, wriggling as you swallowed them. Yet if you were a bat, your verdict might be quite different (Nagel [152]).

Some species have completely different basic requirements to ours. Fish have to be kept in water, many animals have stringent dietary requirements and so on. Consequently, we have to be very careful about assuming that the conditions in which we would suffer are necessarily those in which other species would suffer too. To take an extreme example, it would be a mistake to assess the welfare of tapeworms by trying to answer the question 'How would you like to live inside someone's intestines?' Their "peptic Nirvana" as Julian

Huxley once called it, has nothing to do with the conditions that are best for human welfare, or vice versa.

Medawar [139] gives an illustration of the errors that can result from the well-meaning misuse of this kind of analogy with our own well-being. A little girl he knew found a frog in the garden and her first thought was that it needed warming up because it was cold and dirty. This was a kind thought, but frogs do not flourish at high temperatures. Again, it can be stressed that in order to assess the well-being of animals, we need information about them. We cannot *be* bats or frogs or tapeworms, but we can build up some understanding of what they feel if we find out how the animals themselves react.

Let us follow through the example of the bat. We might observe that bats, when offered the choice, preferred eating live insects to anything else and that insects seemed essential to their health. These observations might alter our views about how bats feel about eating insects. The fact that bats can find their way around in the dark using echolocation might alter the way we thought they feel about living in dark caves and so on. Our picture of what bats feel would not necessarily be accurate, but it would at least be nearer the truth than imagining that bats were just like us, only with wings.

So, we may be able to avoid the worst dangers of putting ourselves in an animal's place by finding out how the animal reacts when put in that place. We then know not just how we react to the idea of being put into a cage, but how a particular animal actually does. Once we can see and hear and measure what the animal does, then we have to contend with the dangers of the other sort of 'analogy with ourselves', that of misinterpreting what it does, which, as we have seen, can in turn be helped by applying the methods discussed in previous chapters.

The value of analogies with ourselves

Having seen the dangers of using analogies with ourselves, we will now emphasize their more positive and useful side. It would be unfortunate if this book had left the impression that finding out about physiology and behaviour was enough to tell us whether animals suffered. For, as we saw in Chapter 2, no amount of measurements can tell us what animals are actually experiencing. Their private mental experiences, if they have them, remain inaccessible to direct observation. All we can do is to use the *in*direct evidence that we have gathered in various ways.

So, if we are to conclude that animals do experience suffering in ways somewhat similar to ourselves, then this conclusion has to be based, in the end, on an analogy with our own feelings. Animals of other species have different physical requirements so the conditions in which they suffer may not be identical to those in which we would. Animals of other species may also have their own ways of expressing themselves, so their 'vocabulary of suffering' may not be the same as ours. But the belief that they suffer, and how much, is based on analogy with ourselves. The belief, for instance, that a frustrated sow is suffering is based on the analogy that we ourselves would suffer if frustrated to the same extent. We would not necessarily be frustrated by the same circumstances and we might show frustration in different ways, but, given the differences between pigs and ourselves, we are still making an analogy.

Are such analogies justified? We will now look at the evidence that has suggested to many people that they are. This evidence comes from physiology, from behaviour and from the probable evolutionary significance of mental experiences.

Physiological evidence on whether other animals suffer in any way like us is probably the least satisfactory, partly because we know so little about the physiological basis of suffering. As discussed in Chapter 5, complex emotions are difficult to tie down to simple physiological variables. Even trying to confine the discussion to physical pain shows how difficult it is to relate what is measured physiologically to what is experienced subjectively (Chapter 3). Thus, pain usually occurs when there is physical injury, but it sometimes occurs with no apparent damage. Conversely, a person may say they feel no pain even when they are severely injured. Some people can tolerate quite easily a treatment that others find intolerably painful and so on. 'Suffering', which is a much more complicated group of emotional states, including, as we have seen, fear and frustration, but also anxiety, bereavement and others we have not discussed, is even more difficult to tie down to particular physiological events. Consequently, it is even more difficult to make the comparison between human beings and other species.

If 'pain' or 'suffering' were simple states, recognizable in human beings by, say, excitation of a particular lump of nervous tissue, it might be feasible to look for corresponding lumps of tissue in other species. Similar patterns of activity might then be used as a basis for saying that similar emotional states were experienced by them. But no such simple basis exists for emotional states. On purely physiological grounds, we would not be able to describe the mental state of another person, let alone that of an animal of another species. All we can say with any certainty is that emotional states in humans seem to be associated with the activation of the nervous system and that the components of the nervous system, the nerve cells, seem to be very similar in all animals that have been looked at. We can also say that there are many similarities in brain structure between ourselves and other mammals, particularly in those areas of the brain, such as the hypothalamus, which are known to be associated with emotions in ourselves (Hubbard [90]). At the very least, as Baker [3], Thorpe [195], and Griffin [70, 71] have argued, this suggests the possibility of some similarity of mental experiences.

A second reason for finding physiological evidence unsatisfactory, however, is that it restricts recognition of suffering to animals that are anatomically and physiologically most like us. It may actually hinder the recognition of suffering in animals which experience similar emotional states, but have different brain structures responsible for them. Just as people of different nationalities can express the same idea in different languages, so animals may be able to experience similar states or perform similar behaviour, with different sorts of nervous systems.

Birds, for example, have rather different brains from mammals. They have a very poorly developed cerebral cortex, an area of the forebrain which is known to be important for learning in mammals. On purely anatomical grounds, therefore, it could easily be concluded that birds could not learn as well as mammals. But this would be quite wrong. Birds equal and sometimes surpass mammals in their abilities to learn (we saw some examples of what they can do in Chapter 2). A different part of the forebrain, the hyperstriatum, seems to be responsible for learning in birds. This has become very large and seems to serve many of the same functions in birds that the cortex does in mammals (Stettner and Matyniak [191]).

In animals such as octopuses that are anatomically even more different from us than are birds, it becomes correspondingly more difficult to decide what an animal can do or experience from what its brain looks like. An octopus can learn complicated tasks, remember what is has learnt for several weeks and so on. Its brain looks very different from that of a mammal, but in a quite uncanny way, its behaviour and learning ability parallel that of birds and mammals (Wells [206]). The behavioural similarity is achieved with a different anatomy. This should lead us to be cautious about placing too much emphasis on structural similarities to humans to tell us whether animals suffer. Details of anatomy may be less important than what the animal actually does. So behavioural evidence for the existence of pain and suffering may be more valuable, particularly for animals that do not look like human beings, a point we will return to in Chapter 10.

In the course of this book, we have looked at many examples of behavioural similarities between man and other species. In Chapter 2, we saw how recent experiments have suggested that animals such as birds may form complex, and very human-like concepts of the world around them. We looked at evidence which suggests that some animals may be aware of what they are doing and how some chimpanzees have mastered some features of sign language. These might be called intellectual similarities. In later chapters, we looked at similarities of emotional responses, such as squeals of pain and struggling to escape from damaging stimuli (Chapter 3), and fear and conflict (Chapter 6). There has been time to mention only some of the similarities that are known.

We have also been stressing all along that pain, feelings of fear, wanting to escape and other forms of suffering are not just accidental nuisances that we, and very probably other animals, happen to be stuck with. On the contrary, they have probably evolved because they helped animals to survive. People without the capacity to feel pain, for instance, often burn, bruise and lacerate themselves during childhood. They may chew their own tongues when they eat and have to learn, often with great effort, not to keep wounding themselves (Melzack [140]). So feeling pain, although unpleasant at the time, is clearly an advantage. A similar argument can be made for other unpleasant emotions that we call suffering. At some level, for instance, fear is a helpful mechanism (Chapter 6) in that it acts as an advance warning that injury will occur unless some action is taken.

It is not only human beings that have developed mechanisms for avoiding injury, escaping from harmful conditions and so on. It seems unlikely, therefore, that it would only be in human beings that these mechanisms involve subjective experiences to accompany the physiological and behavioural events that occur.

Griffin [70] argues that conscious awareness is of considerable evolutionary advantage. Being aware of what is going on, he argues, is a help in simulating the future and generally 'understanding' the world. Because of the widespread advantages of conscious awareness, Griffin believes that it is very likely that many animals besides human beings are conscious of what goes on around them. This argument is particularly plausible when applied to subjective feelings such as those involved in escaping or evading danger. The behaviour and biological needs are there in many species. As Hume [94] points out, it is reasonable to suggest that at least some of the same subjective feelings are there too.

Analogies with ourselves thus occupy a peculiar position in the assessment of animal suffering. For many people they are at the very root of the belief that animals do suffer in ways somewhat like ourselves. Often, the origins of this belief are not clear, but it grows out of the conviction that there are great similarities, physiological and behavioural, between humans and at least some other species. However, as we have seen, if *all* we had to go on were analogies with ourselves, we would not have a very clear picture of what animal suffering is like. Animals vary. They are not all like human beings. Some of them are very different, some of them, like octopuses, could almost be described as science fiction animals. So we have, temporarily, to abandon analogies with ourselves and try to devise ways of finding out about animal suffering from the animal's point of view. We have looked at what some of these ways might be and how science can help us to understand even something as elusive as animal suffering.

Then, when all the evidence has been accumulated, we have to return again to analogies with ourselves for the final verdict. Because mental events cannot be measured directly, we need analogies to make the final link between behaviour and physiology on the one hand and mental events on the other.

It is important to stress, however, that they are very different analogies from the initial ones. They are analogies disciplined by scientific method and informed about the biological needs of the animals. The effort of finding scientific ways of studying animal suffering is not made unnecessary just because, in the end, we need analogies with ourselves. For those analogies are now strengthened and far more likely to yield an accurate picture of what an animal is feeling than uninformed analogies ever could.

It takes a certain amount of humility to accept that other

animals besides ourselves may suffer and feel pain. Here drawing analogies with ourselves can be most valuable. But it takes even more humility to recognize that the subjective experiences of other species may not be exactly, or even remotely like our own. Here analogies with ourselves may be misleading unless firmly tied to evidence from all possible sources about those other species. The message of this book has been that we should be humble enough to try to collect that evidence.

9 Conclusions

We have now looked at each of the main ways in which people have tried to judge whether animals are suffering or not. The general tone may have seemed rather negative. Each method has told us something, but each one has been criticised. Uncovering the weaknesses of each method is, however, much more constructive than it might seem at first. It is necessary to be aware of the limitations of your materials before you start building a house. This particular house — a picture of what the subjective worlds of animals might be like — is a very difficult one to construct (Chapter 2). At the risk of being repetitive, it is worth saying once again that we cannot have direct evidence of the subjective experiences of any other beings, human or otherwise. All we have as building blocks are fallible pieces of indirect evidence. The house is most likely to remain standing if these are put together carefully, with the weak points in one kind of evidence buttressed by evidence from another source. For example, a weakness of preference tests as a means for evaluating welfare is, as we have seen, that animals do not necessarily choose what is best for their physical health in the long run. Preference tests should, therefore, not be used alone, but taken together with evidence about what is known to be best for the animal's health.

The purpose of this chapter is house-building. We will attempt to tackle the difficult task of drawing up guidelines for assessing whether an animal is suffering. As the recommendations will be based on methods discussed in previous chapters, we will first briefly review the conclusions from each one.

We saw in Chapter 3 that *physical health* and *productivity* are widely used criteria for assessing the welfare of animals. These two should be kept separate. *Productivity* is a dangerous criterion since it may be used to refer to the profitability of a whole commercial unit, such as a chicken farm. A farm can tolerate damage and even death of some individual animals without profits necessarily falling. Giving each animal more space or installing new cages might improve the health and output of each animal, but still not be economically worthwhile. In other words, both physical and mental suffering may occur in profitable farm units.

Physical health of individual animals, on the other hand, is a very valuable criterion for assessing welfare. Disease and injury are major causes of suffering. Their absence is a necessary part of any animal's well-being. Nevertheless, animals may still suffer despite an external appearance of good health. Doubts about the physical health criterion thus centre not so much on its usefulness as an indicator of welfare as on whether it is the *only* method that need be applied. The occurrence of physiological and behavioural disturbances in apparently healthy animals suggest that other methods of assessing suffering should be looked for.

A very important source of evidence on animal suffering is often assumed to be the behaviour of *animals in the wild*. In Chapter 4 we discussed the use of comparisons between animals in restricted environments with those of the same species in wild or semi-wild conditions. It is very tempting to see a natural life as a life free from suffering, to see Nature, as it were, through Rousseau-tinted spectacles. But life in the wild may be very harsh. There may also be genetic and environmentally produced differences between wild and domesticated animals which make comparisons between them difficult to interpret. What is a more serious objection is that there is no evidence that a difference in the behaviour of free and restricted animals *in itself* shows that the restricted ones are suffering. The main function of such comparative studies is to indicate where the differences are and where, therefore, particular attention should be paid to the possibility that suffering is occurring. At this stage it is only a possibility. Whether suffering is actually occurring has to be established by independent means.

These independent means include the physical health of the animals (which may often be better in captive animals than in wild ones) and *physiological measurements* such as heart rate and hormone levels which we discussed in Chapter 5. The problem here was to decide how much of a physiological change an animal can tolerate before we say that it is suffering. Many physiological changes occur as quite normal features of an animal's daily life. They are indications that the animal's body is functioning properly. Some degree of 'stress' seems to be beneficial to animals. Another difficulty is that complex emotions that come under the heading of 'suffering' are not easily related to the simple physiological measurements that can be made at the moment. On a more practical level, physiological measurements can be criticised because they involve interfering with the animal, perhaps giving it a minor operation. Technological improvements such as tiny radio transmitters for signalling physiological changes may overcome some of the difficulties. But at the moment, physiological measurements of welfare are limited by the twin problems of what to measure and how to relate what is measured to whether the animal is suffering.

It has also been suggested that an animal's suffering might be recognized through its *behaviour*, without the disadvantages of having to make damaging physiological measurements. In Chapter 6 we discussed the various problems of trying to do this. 'Abnormal' behaviour patterns have been described in a number of animals in restricted conditions, such as zoos and farms. Here again, the problem is to know how much abnormality has to be shown to justify the statement that the animal is suffering. The word 'abnormal' is a very emotive one and is used to describe many different categories of behaviour. Some abnormal behaviour is clearly indicative of suffering as it leads to actual physical damage to the animal. But other behaviour which has also been described as abnormal is part of the animal's natural repertoire. Fear, frustration and aggression, for example, occur in unrestricted animals although they may occur more often when the animals are confined. There is thus a similar problem to that which exists with physiological measurements. How much of a particular behaviour must an animal do before it can be said to be suffering? The potential of behaviour as an indicator of suffering is very great, but with the knowledge we have at present, it is not always possible to know how much behaviour corresponds to how much suffering.

In Chapter 7, we discussed a more direct method for trying to see the world from the animal's point of view. This was to give animals the opportunity to *choose* for themselves which environments they prefer and to show what they find positively or negatively *reinforcing*. Unfortunately, animals do not always choose what is best for them. They may also choose differently depending on the time when they are tested and their previous experience. So such an approach needs careful interpretation. Nevertheless, without the use of words, it is the closest we can come to being able to ask an animal what it is feeling.

Finally, in Chapter 8, we discussed another widely used method for assessing the mental well-being of animals, that of using *ourselves as models* of what animals might feel. The conviction that it is possible to draw an analogy between suffering in ourselves and that in other species is probably the basis for people's concern about animal welfare in the first place. But the conviction that all we need to do to understand animals is to look into ourselves is also the basis for a lot of error. Many animals are very different from human beings. They have different requirements for food and living conditions. To judge an animal's environment in terms of what we ourselves like or dislike is a well-meaning but misguided standard. Ultimately, as we have no direct access to the mental experiences of other species, we need to draw on analogies with ourselves to conclude that animals suffer. Such analogies should, however, be drawn only with the help of all possible evidence about the animals concerned, such as that derived by the methods discussed in earlier chapters.

These, then, are the basic components. We now have to consider the ways in which the results of each method for assessing suffering might be put together to produce a final picture of what an animal is experiencing. As we do this, it is important to bear in mind that the question of how to recognize animal suffering is quite distinct from that of whether we should tolerate or condemn it. As we saw in Chapter 1, these two questions often become confused. Exactly what people mean be 'suffering' often depends on whether they think animal suffering is necessary or unnecessary (for example, to produce food or medicines). The question of whether causing animals to suffer is justified under at least some conditions is an important one. But we are not concerned with it at the moment. Our concern here is strictly with how to recognize suffering.

Throughout this book, we have taken 'suffering' to mean the experience of a wide range of unpleasant subjective states. Within this we have distinguished pain, an acute form of suffering recognizable by signs such as struggling, squealing and so on from longer lasting states of suffering. We have paid particular attention to that caused by fear, frustration and conflict, but only because these have been most extensively studied. Other possible states of suffering which we have not considered include those caused by loss of social companions, anxiety and so on.

We have seen that one of the most important things to know before deciding whether an animal is suffering is whether the animal is physically healthy. In many cases, we simply do not yet have basic factual information about the physical health of the animals for which we are concerned. One of the most urgent needs in the whole field of animal welfare is for quantitative surveys on all aspects of the physical conditions of animals, particularly animals in the much criticised intensive farms and research laboratories. Such surveys would not in themselves settle the issue of whether the animals were suffering, but they would be a great step forward. We might at least all agree what we are talking about. We would have cleared the first hurdle for assessing an animal's welfare and could then go on to apply other criteria.

Imagine some hypothetical animals kept permanently in small cages. People have expressed concern about their welfare. However, the animals appear to be very healthy. They are frequently inspected for signs of injury or disease, but none is found. What could then be done to assess their welfare?

A first step might be to document the differences in behaviour, physiology and general appearance between the hypothetical animals and animals of the same species kept in less restricted or even wild conditions. There might be very major differences. The wild animals might show a whole range of behaviour patterns not seen at all in the caged ones. Conversely, the caged ones might show 'abnormal' behaviour which was completely lacking in their wild cousins. There would thus be some omissions and some additions to the behavioural repertoire of the caged animals. To decide which, if any, of these indicated suffering, a number of physiological and behavioural studies could be done. These would show the likely causes of the unusual behaviour of the caged animals, whether it was due to frustration, for example, and whether this was accompanied by any physiological disturbances likely to lead to 'stress' diseases.

Finally, the caged animals could be tested to see what environment they preferred. In this case, let us assume that they preferred their cages over any other environment, even after extensive testing and familiarization with freer conditions.

At the end of all this we might be able to say that the animals were in good physical health, but that they showed a number of unusual behaviour patterns associated with captivity. These unusual behaviour patterns, however, appeared not to indicate that the animals were suffering. The animals did not appear to be frustrated or frightened and most of the differences appeared to be due to the positive reactions of the animals to their keepers, rather in the way that domestic dogs show behaviour towards humans that would not be seen in wild counterparts. The animals also appeared to 'like' their cages, because they chose them in preference to conditions which naive humans had thought they would prefer.

The final verdict in this hypothetical case might be that although the animals were being kept in conditions very different from the natural habitat of their wild ancestors, all the evidence pointed to the conclusion that their welfare was good. The animals might not, under any criteria, appear to be suffering.

On the other hand, of course, the conclusions might have been very different, even given high standards of physical health. If the animals had shown evidence of a high degree of frustration, for example, prolonged over much of their lives, with evidence of a build up of physiological symptoms that were known to be the precursers of disease even though the animals were still apparently healthy, we might conclude that they were suffering. If, in addition they showed every sign of trying to escape from their cages and avoiding them when given the opportunity, the evidence that they were suffering would be even stronger.

The point of these speculative examples is to show how, given different sorts of evidence, different conclusions would be reached about whether the animals were suffering. It is possible to summarize the arguments by drawing up a tentative check-list or programme for deciding whether a particular treatment of animals which may be under suspicion is really responsible for making animals suffer. The following questions will help to make such a decision:

(1) *What are the conditions under which the animals are kept?* The answer to this question should include information not just on long-term living conditions, but also details of treatment which may last only a short time, such as capture, medical treatment, transport, mutilations such as tail-docking, experimental procedures and so on. It should also give a quantitative idea of the range of conditions that are

involved, for instance, the numbers of animals kept at different stocking densities, the effects of good and bad stockmanship and the risks associated with fire, breakdown of mechanical apparatus and so on. It is, in short, essential to know exactly what happens to how many animals.

(2) *Are the animals physically healthy?* Again, the answer must be expressed quantitatively, not by picking out unrepresentative examples. It should include information on the general condition of the animals, any signs of specific disease or injury or general signs of ill-health as listed for that species.

(3) *Does the behaviour, physiology and general appearance of the animals differ from that of genetically similar animals in less restricted conditions?*

(4) *Is there evidence of severe physiological disturbance?* In particular, it should be established whether the physiological state of the animals is such that, were it to be prolonged, the animals would probably develop 'stress' diseases.

(5) *What is the cause of the behavioural differences established under (3)?* Are they due to frustration, for example? If so, is the frustration long lasting? Does the animal show behaviour which is known to be the precurser of pathologically abnormal behaviour such as self-mutilation?

(6) *What conditions do the animals themselves prefer?*

This set of questions cannot be answered without a great deal of factual information about each type of animal and the ways that they are treated. The questions may, however, give some idea of where more research is needed and of how the results might be expected to fit in to the final evaluation of animal welfare.

Inevitably, this evaluation will contain a subjective element. There is a subjective element, for example, in deciding how much fear, conflict etc. constitutes 'suffering'. There is no simple way of deciding how much weight should be given to the various questions listed above. There is, unfortunately, no formula for giving a clear yes/no answer to the question of whether an animal is suffering; that must in the end be based on analogies with our own feelings. However, the point of this book is not to eliminate subjective judgements altogether from our analysis of whether animals are suffering. The point has been to put those judgements on a scientific footing and to base them on biological knowledge of the animals concerned.

10   *Stumbling blocks and stepping stones*

It may seem odd to have another chapter after the conclusions. The reason for it is that the conclusions were about methods for assessing suffering, and these, as we saw in Chapter 1, are only part of the total picture of animal welfare. Having focused for most of the book on such methods, we will now move the camera backwards, as it were, and try to take a wider view. Controversies rage. Governments are under pressure to change the laws on the treatment of animals. Scientists are on the defensive over their experiments on animals. Farmers are criticised. But most people go on eating animals, demanding that the products that they eat or wear are tested, wanting better drugs or transplants or vaccines to save their lives.

By coming to some conclusions about methods for recognizing suffering, therefore, we have only just begun. There is a long way to go before reaching any final overall conclusions about the treatment of animals. This book cannot take us all the way. It is a guide to only a small part of the journey. But this final chapter will attempt to provide some stepping stones for the way ahead, by examining some of the difficulties over which people most often stumble in debates about animal welfare.

'What about plants and "lower" animals?'

A difficulty raised by many people is that of where to draw the line. If it is thought that animals such as chimpanzees and pigs can suffer, how do we know that, say, apple-trees do not?

This difficulty is sometimes used to ridicule a concern for animal welfare on the grounds that once you start caring about some animals, you are then committed to giving equal weight to the suffering of all animals and plants, unless you make very arbitrary distinctions between different sorts of organisms. The arbitrariness of the distinctions is ridiculed and, with it, a concern for animal welfare.

Now there is nothing necessarily invalid about making somewhat arbitrary distinctions between different sorts of organisms. There is no clear cut-off point between youth and old age, or between night and day. But this does not mean that there is no difference between the extremes. Similarly, the fact that we may not be certain exactly where to draw the line does not invalidate the basic idea that some organisms can suffer greatly and others much less or not at all. We should not, therefore, give up caring for animals just because our care may have to have limits and we may not be certain exactly where those limits should be set.

In other walks of life, we accept arbitrary distinctions all the time. Most people agree, for example, that it is a good thing to have some sort of speed limit in built up areas. 70 mph would be much too fast. 5 mph would be much too slow. As Glover [68] points out, the actual limit of 30 mph is arbitrary in the sense that there is no evidence that a limit of 31 mph or 29 mph would not be just as effective.

There are various ways in which people have tried to deal with the problem of deciding which organisms they should care about and which they should care less about. Some of these are internally consistent but others, as we shall see, are much less so. The most radical way of drawing the line is to be equally concerned for the welfare of anything that is alive. This, however, puts cabbages on the same moral footing as whales and humans, and is therefore a view that most people find quite untenable. Rather less extreme is the idea that we should take account of the welfare of an organism if there is evidence that it can *suffer*. This is argued by Ryder [169], Singer [185] and Brophy [19], amongst others. The capacity to suffer is usually linked to the possession of a nervous system, which therefore excludes plants. However, the arguments over whether plants can suffer have recently been obscured by recent claims that plants do have emotions and feelings.

Tompkins and Bird [201], in a book called *The Secret Life of Plants*, argued that because some records of electrical activity in plants looked like those from people linked up to lie detectors, plants therefore had thought-processes and feelings like people. They credited plants with being able to respond to human thoughts and emotions and to distant events such as the injury or death of another organism. If true, such claims would have been quite revolutionary. They would have altered our whole view of eating apples or cutting down trees. But carefully controlled experiments have totally failed to reproduce the results on which the book was based. Galston and Slayman [65] argue that the original results were a complete artefact and that misleading results were obtained because of a faulty connection in the circuit used for making the measurements.

Emotion seems to be a property of a highly developed nervous system. No plant has a structure which has anything like the complexity of an insect or even a jellyfish. As well as this, plants show no behavioural evidence of suffering or trying to escape. A plant does not uproot itself and run away or try to shake off someone who is cutting off one of its branches. It does not have muscles or a nervous system to control movement. In animals, as we have seen repeatedly, suffering and pain seem to have evolved because they aid survival, forming part of the animals' escape mechanisms or their capacity to learn from past experience. We would thus not expect that suffering would evolve in organisms such as plants which cannot escape or do anything about their predicaments. The link between a nervous system, active movement and suffering is, of course, speculative, but it is functionally plausible and it provides a basis for believing that animals can suffer without having to attribute emotions to the whole plant kingdom as well.

For many people, this, too, is unsatisfactory. It seems to

imply that as much weight should be given to the suffering of an insect as to that of a mammal, since both have complex nervous systems. Should we, then, see swatting flies or leaving them to die slowly on fly papers as no different from clubbing baby seals? If there is a difference, what is it?

A very common view of this problem is to try to make a distinction between 'higher' and 'lower' animals and to argue that only 'higher' animals suffer. There are two major difficulties with this. One is that there is no generally agreed definition of what constitutes 'higher' or 'lower' animals and the other is that, almost whatever definition is used, there is no obvious connection between being 'higher' and suffering. Thus, a 'lower' animal may, amongst other things, mean one that is the ancestor of a 'higher' one, or one that resembles their common ancestor most, or an animal that is simpler, or one that is stupider, or most frequently of all, one that does not resemble a human being as much as a 'higher' animal. Most people mean some unspecified mixture of all of these. But this is very confusing because these various attributes do not have any necessary connection with each other let alone with 'suffering' . For example, octopuses do not resemble human beings and in no sense are they ancestral to them. They have been evolving quite independently from the line that eventually gave rise to human beings for at least 600 million years. On these grounds, they would be counted as 'lower' animals. Yet, they have a complex nervous system and, as we saw in Chapter 8, almost mammal-like powers of learning and memory, so that on this basis, they might be counted as 'higher' animals.

The basic objection to any lower/higher distinction is that evolution did not take place along just one pathway or ladder. Different groups of animals evolved along their own ladders. Birds and mammals, for example, were both evolving at the same time, from quite separate groups of reptiles. Both, in their own ways, achieved 'heights' of learning ability, control over body temperature and so on. Similarly, some insects show a 'high' degree of social organization that evolved quite separately from the social behaviour of mammals. Since different attributes can arise separately in different groups, there is no reason to suppose that an animal which is 'higher' as far as one attribute is concerned is going to be 'higher' for any others. In other words, as Hodos and Campbell [84], amongst others, have argued, the terms 'higher' and 'lower' animals are extremely confusing. For this reason they are unhelpful guides to whether an animal is capable of suffering.

They are particularly misleading when 'higher' is equated with 'human-like', because the implication is then that only human beings are capable of suffering, or at least that only human suffering matters in a moral sense. Many people do in fact subscribe to the view that the boundary between different sorts of organisms should be drawn not between animals and plants or between different sorts of non-human animals, but firmly between humans and all other species. They believe that human beings are uniquely important, a view that has been called 'speciesism' by Ryder [169] to emphasize the parallel with racism. It is important to distinguish two sorts of speciesism as they have somewhat different consequences. One is pure speciesism or speciesism without a reason. The other is speciesism with a reason. Pure speciesism means discriminating against other species simply because they are not human. For example, a pure speciesist would regard a human embryo, even one at a very early stage of development, as more worthy of moral consideration than an intelligent adult chimpanzee, because one is a member of the human species and the other is not. However clever an animal of another species might be, or however much it could suffer the pure speciesist would always regard its suffering as less important than that of any human being.

'Speciesism with a reason', on the other hand, means discriminating against other species because they lack some attribute which humans have and which, by implication, means that their suffering is less important. For example, suppose that someone believed that people deserved special attention because they have highly developed speech. He might point out that only humans have this capacity and use this as a basis for making a moral distinction between humans and all other animals. If another species were then shown to have the capacity of speech, the rational speciesist would presumably have to admit that species into the 'human' category. Whether he would do so or whether he would then change his criterion would be a test of whether his speciesism was, in fact, rational.

As Singer [185] argues, the problem with speciesism, even speciesism with a reason, is to justify the reason. The difference between human beings and other species which is singled out has to be shown to be relevant to the moral question of how they ought to be treated. If, for example, one is arguing that the capacity to suffer should be the basis of extending moral considerations to an organism, then the difference has to be shown to have something to do with suffering. Take a quite ridiculous example to illustrate this point. Imagine someone who was a speciesist of a rather wierd sort: he discriminated against all animals except goats. His attitude would provoke the obvious question 'Why goats?'. This speciesist has a reason: 'Because they have horns'. This is clearly an unsatisfactory argument unless he can tell us why having horns has anything to do with the way goats should be treated and why he refuses to behave in a similar way towards other horned animals such as cows.

By using this example, we can see the difficulties that occur with commonly used speciesist arguments: humans are given special moral consideration by most people, sometimes just because they are human, but sometimes because they are different in some way from other animals. It is not enough, however, just to point to *a* difference, even a difference which marks humans out as 'better' or 'higher' in some respect. The difference has to be shown to be relevant to the ways we feel that humans and other animals *ought* to be treated, for example, how much they suffer. Being human or human-like or 'higher' is an unreliable guide to whether an animal experiences suffering. If we want to know whether it does, we should go directly to the physiological and behavioural evidence, using methods such as the ones we have discussed in earlier chapters.

'Aren't animals nasty to each other?'

Another difficulty that many people encounter arises from what they see as animals causing suffering to each other. As was described in Chapter 4, for example, hyenas kill their prey by tearing it limb from limb. Insects such as digger wasps paralyse their prey without killing it and then lay an egg on it. This means that when the larva hatches, it eats an immobilized but still living insect. Why should anyone be concerned for the welfare of animals when they, in turn, are often so 'cruel' to their victims? Do people who are concerned about animal welfare have a double moral standard, one for themselves and one for other animals? They seem to be saying that something can be described as cruel when a human does it to an animal, but not when that animal does something very similar to another animal (Brophy [19]).

Once again, there are various ways in which people have approached the dilemma. Brophy [19] admits that she simply does not know the answer to it, beyond thinking herself morally superior to her cat and deciding not to treat her cat as unkindly as her cat treats birds. A few peple have taken the extreme view and advocated that there should be no double standard. They believe that wild animals should be prevented from killing or maiming their prey. Horrified by television films of the way that hunting dogs hunt their prey, they have gone so far as to suggest that such animals should be penned up and fed only on humanely killed meat.

Yet other people have taken refuge in the belief that animals only kill when it is 'necessary' (for food, for example). They distinguish this from 'unnecessary' killing that humans often do (as in sport). Unfortunately, this distinction cannot always be maintained. Kruuk [120] describes how foxes go in for orgies of killing for no apparent reason. In a gull-colony or hen-house, for instance, they may kill far more than they can eat or carry or hide away.

It is, in fact, extremely difficult to make a clear moral distinction between what animals do to other animals and what people do to animals. One is 'natural', it may be objected, the other is not. But both may cause equal suffering. Consider the difficulties of making moral distinctions in one area which has recently received quite a lot of publicity: the scientific study of the way animals kill each other.

To understand the way animals live in the wild, it may be necessary to find out about the way in which they kill their prey. If a scientist stands and watches what happens, few people would condemn him (although some would). If he examines the carcasses left behind when a fox has raided a gull colony, there would probably be few protests. But what is the position if he goes a stage further than this? Instead of just watching passively, he might interfere in some way, perhaps by releasing a tame hawk near a flock of pigeons to see how they react to each other. Is this cruel? He might wish to study the hunting behaviour of the hawk at closer quarters. He might build a large aviary and release both pigeons and a hawk into it. Is he now being cruel? Even if the hawk kills one of the pigeons, this is an event which happens often enough in the wild. But at what point does a scientist cease to be an observer and become responsible for 'cruelty', when that 'cruelty' is inflicted not by him but by other animals? As Macdonald and I [135] have argued, there are no hard and fast lines, no easy answers to such questions.

Sociobiology and animal welfare

There is a sinister version of the 'nasty animals' dilemma which is sometimes used to justify any sort of exploitation or ill-treatment of other species. This is that as we ourselves are animals, we too have been evolved to exploit other species. It is sometimes thought that a discipline called sociobiology tells us that we are selfish and that the exploitation of our own and other species is 'in our genes'. Caring about the welfare of animals is, on this view, contrary to Nature, which is seen as 'red in tooth and claw'.

There are two quite different replies to this. The first is that even a view of nature red in tooth and claw has to leave room for the formation of social groups and partnerships between animals, even members of different species, as these undoubtedly occur. We have already come across the partnership between large fish, such as Butterfly fish and Groupers and much smaller 'cleaner fish' which eat the parasites clinging to their skin and gills. The cleaner fish often go inside the mouth and gills of the large fish, but they do not get eaten, even though they are a suitable size for a meal. On the contrary, the large fish often give special signals to their cleaners that they are just about to close their mouths and then move off. They may even defend their cleaners against other fish. This is not, however, pure altruism on the part of the larger fish. Trivers [202] has suggested how the habit might have evolved. Reliable cleaners, like reliable hairdressers, are hard to find. The big fish return again and again to particular cleaners to have their parasites removed. There is mutual benefit. The small fish gets food and the large ones are cleaned. It does not appear to be in the large fish's best interests to spoil the relationship by eating the cleaner, even at the end of a cleaning session, and then having to search for another.

In other words, co-operation and mutual assistance between animals of different species can, and does, occur. But according to most biologists, this only happens when each side gets something out of the partnership as in the case of the cleaner fish and their clients. Does this mean that we would be genetically incapable of caring about the welfare of other animals unless we ourselves obtain some benefit, such as caring for our farm animals because they, in turn, will benefit us? Does sociobiology rule out the possibility of caring for animals unless there is something in it for us?

The second reply to the 'sociobiology' argument makes it clear that sociobiology does not really tell us anything at all about animal welfare. Sociobiology, for all its new name, is not in fact a new discipline at all. It is an amalgam of much older studies, particularly those of the behaviour of animals in their natural environments. Tinbergen [198] long ago stressed the importance of studying animals in the wild and trying to understand the evolutionary significance of behaviour – how behaviour helps animals to survive. He saw an animal's behaviour as subject to natural selection in the same way as its shape or its colouring and this is a basic tenet of sociobiology. A belief that behaviour has evolved implies that genes are having some influence on the behaviour. Otherwise natural selection would not work (since the survival of the fittest implies that there are some genetic differences between the fittest and the less fit. Unless the differences were at least partly inherited by the offspring, the beneficial traits would not be passed on to the next generation and no evolution would occur).

But believing that there is *some genetic influence* is quite different from believing that there is *complete genetic control*. There are many cases where known genetic effects can be partly or completely obscured by environmental influences. For example, the condition known as PKU in humans is due to a genetic defect. Affected individuals lack an enzyme which converts one amino acid, phenylalanine into another, tyrosine. The result is that phenylalanine accumulates in the brain and causes severe mental retardation. Although this is a genetic defect, it can be almost completely overcome by feeding affected children from infancy on a diet which does not contain phenylalanine (Parsons [154]). Similarly, genetic differences between strains of mice can be largely overcome by experience during their own lifetimes. Lagerspetz [126] showed that genetically aggressive mice could be made much less aggressive by the experience of fighting a very aggressive opponent, and Cooper and Zubeck [33] showed that genetic differences between bright and dull rats could be completely eliminated by environmental factors such as the complexities of the rearing cages.

Contrary to what many people believe, sociobiology does not tell us that our genes determine what we do in any absolute or irrevocable way. Even if natural selection is a ruthless process, favouring selfishness over altriusm, this does not mean that we are therefore condemned to being selfish towards our own or other species. We do not have to follow what our genes 'tell' us, because, as the examples above illustrate, genetic effects can be overcome. What we choose to do towards other animals is up to us. It is not dictated by our evolutionary history. The fault, if there is one, is not in our genes. 'Sociobiology' cannot be used as an argument against animal welfare.

Reduction or abolition?

Yet another difficulty which many people encounter is that of thinking that concern for animal welfare has to be all or nothing. They feel that it is hypocritical to say that you care about the suffering of animals unless you are prepared to give up eating meat altogether, have no medicines which are based on animal products or animal tests, never kill an animal even if it is responsible for spreading disease and so on. Because they find such an extreme position unthinkable, many people feel that it is unrealistic to care about the welfare of animals. They may be contemptuous of vegetarians who wear leather shoes or of someone who campaigns for fewer animal experiments while stopping short of a complete ban. Their attitude rests on the assumption that unless you can abolish all suffering, there is no point in trying to reduce the amount of suffering at all. This is a curious attitude to take, because if one believes that causing intense and prolonged suffering to animals is wrong, even a small reduction in suffering must be better than no reduction at all.

Russell and Burch [168] for example, believed that it was neither possible nor even desirable to abolish all cruel practices at once and they advocated instead a programme for lessening the amount of suffering caused. They put forward what they called the 3 Rs for the humane treatment of animals, which they originally proposed for the use of animals in scientific experiments but which are just as applicable to other areas of animal welfare. Their 3 Rs were Replacement, by which they meant finding alternatives to methods which caused suffering either by not using animals at all or by using them in ways which did not cause them distress; Reduction in the numbers of animals used; and Refinement which meant making sure that, if suffering had to be caused, it was kept to a minimum. These 3 Rs are not the same as a total ban, but if they were followed, a considerable improvement could be made in the well-being of many animals.

These are just a few of the many difficulties that come up again and again in arguments about animal welfare. There are many more which we could have considered, but these will give some idea of the complexity of the issues involved. We will end the chapter by drawing together some threads and looking briefly at the main problem areas.

Issues of animal welfare

In this book, we have seen that decisions about the way animals should be treated involve at least three stages. Firstly, there is the stage of finding out what actually happens to animals – how they are kept at various stages in their lives, how many animals are involved and what exactly happens to them. This is no easy task, but it is quite essential to all subsequent arguments.

Secondly, there is the stage of accumulating evidence about whether what is done to animals causes them to suffer. This, too, is difficult and may mean doing a great deal more research than has yet been attempted. It involves looking at the behaviour, health and physiology of the animals and arriving at an assessment of their mental state along the lines suggested in the previous chapter.

Finally comes the decision of what to do about the animals, whether to pass laws and whether to condemn conditions that cause suffering or to condone them because they are thought necessary for some purpose. This involves careful consideration of the consequences of any proposed changes. It is impossible to take a stand against a practice which we believe causes animals to suffer and leave it at that. The welfare of animals cannot be seen in isolation because changes in the treatment of animals, particularly those backed up by the law, have enormous consequences. They could change what we eat, what we wear, the kinds of medicines available and even whether a treatment for a particular disease is available at all. They could affect the course of scientific research through legislation about what scientists are and are not permitted to do. Changes in the way that farm animals are kept could affect the availability and price of food. Changes in the way that animals are used in research could mean that drugs are not tested on any other living animal before being given to human beings. Not controlling pest animals could affect the spread of diseases, the amount of food there is to feed the human population and so on. This book has not attempted to make up anyone's mind for them, simply to suggest a few guidelines. I hope it has made a few people stop and think. These are the issues I hope they will think about:

I *Farming*. The World Federation for the Protection of Animals [23] estimates that, excluding poultry, 1000 million animals are killed each year to provide meat. The husbandry, transportation and ultimate slaughter of food animals is a primary concern of animal welfare.

II. *Biomedical uses of animals*. The WFPA [23] estimates that, throughout the world, some 140 million animals are used for research each year, these being mostly rats, mice, hamsters and guinea-pigs. But large numbers of dogs, cats and monkeys are also used. Of particular public concern is the experimental use of animals, but non-experimental uses such as the preparation of vaccines may cause suffering, too. Vertebrate animals usually arouse more concern than invertebrates, which often have little or no legal protection.

III. *Wildlife*. Areas of concern include hunting animals for sport, the control of pest animals by such means as poisoning, snaring etc., and the capture and transport of wild animals as pets and for zoos, and safari parks.

Each of these issues is extremely complicated and deserves

a book on its own. But by now I hope it will be clear that before we can translate a concern for any of these issues into effective action, we need three things. We need information about how animals are treated, we need biological knowledge about the animals themselves, and we need a clear evaluation of the likely consequences of our action.

Without this basic preparation, we may see suffering where there is none or, worse, overlook it because it does not have a human face.

References

1. Archer, J. (1979) *Animals under Stress*. Edward Arnold, London.

2. Baerends, G. P. and Kruijt, J. P. (1973) Stimulus selection. In *Constraints on Learning*, edited by R. A. Hinde and J. Stevenson-Hinde, p. 23. Academic Press, London.

3. Baker, J. R. (1948) *The Scientific Basis of Kindness to Animals*. Universities Federation for Animal Welfare.

4. Baldwin, B. A. and Ingram, D. L. (1967) Behavioural thermoregulation in pigs. *Physiology and Behaviour* **2**, 15.

5. Baldwin, B. A. and Meese, G. B. (1977) Sensory reinforcement and illumination preference in the domesticated pig. *Animal Behaviour* **25**, 497.

6. Baldwin, B. A. and Stephens, D. B. (1973) The effect of conditioned behaviour and environmental factors on plasma cortico steroid levels in pigs. *Physiology and Behaviour* **10**, 267.

7. Bareham, J. R. (1972) Effects of cages and semi-intensive deep-litter pens on the behaviour, adrenal response and production of two strains of laying hens. *British Veterinary Journal* **128**, 153.

8. Bareham, J. R. (1976) A comparison of the behaviour and production of laying hens in experimental and conventional battery cages. *Applied Animal Ethology* **2**, 291.

9. Barnett, S. A. (1964) Social stress. In *Viewpoints in Biology*, Vol. 3, edited by J. D. Carthy and C. L. Duddington. Butterworths, London.

10. Bateson, P. P. G. (1980) Discontinuities in developmental changes in the organisation of play in cats. In *Behavioural Development*, edited by K. Immelmann, G. W. Barlow, M. Main and L. Petrinovich, in press. Cambridge University Press.

11. Beebe, W. (1937) *Pheasants, their Lives and Homes*. Robert Hale, London.

12. Beninger, R. J., Kendall, S. B. and Vanderwolf, C. H. (1974) The ability of rats to discriminate their own behaviours. *Canadian Journal of Psychology* **28**, 79.

13. Berkson, G. (1967) Abnormal stereotyped acts. In *Comparative Psychopathology*, edited by J. Zubin and H. F. Hunt, p. 76. Grune and Stratton, New York.

14. Bolles, R. C. (1967) *Theory of Motivation*. Harper and Row, New York.

15. Bowman, J. C. (1968) Production characters in poultry. In *Genetics and Animal Breeding*, edited by I. Johansson and J. Rendel, p. 340. Oliver and Boyd, Edinburgh.

16. Brady, J. V. (1975) Conditioning and emotion. In *Emotions – their Parameters and Measurements*, edited by L. Levi, p. 309. Raven Press, New York.

17. Brambell, F. W. R. (1965) Chairman. Report of the Technical Committee to Enquire into the Welfare of Animals kept under Intensive Livestock Husbandry Systems. Cmnd 2836. H.M.S.O., London.

18. Broadhurst, P. L. (1960) Abnormal animal behaviour. In *Handbook of Abnormal Psychology*, edited by H. J. Eysenck, p. 726. Pitman, London.

19. Brophy, B. (1979) The Darwinist's dilemma. In *Animals' Rights – a Symposium*, edited by D. Paterson and R. D. Ryder, p. 63. Centaur Press, London.

20. Brown, P. L. (1974) The synthesis of the stress entity. *British Veterinary Journal* **130**, 93.

21. Candland, D. K., Taylor, D. B., Dresdale, L., Leiphart, J. M. and Solow, S. P. (1969) Heart rate, aggression and dominance in the domestic chicken. *Journal of Comparative and Physiological Psychology* **67**, 70.

22. Cannon, W. B. (1929) *Bodily Changes in Pain, Hunger, Fear and Rage; an Account of Recent Researches into the Function of Emotional Excitement*. 2nd edn. Appleton, New York.

23. Carding, T. (1974) Work at the international level for animal protection. *Animalia* **1**, 3.

24. Casey, K. L. (1978) Problem of defining pain. In *Pain*, Neurosciences Research Program Bulletin Vol. 16 (1), edited by F. W. L. Kerr and K. L. Casey. MIT Press, Chicago.

25. Central Office of Information Reference Pamphlet No. 43 (1977) *Agriculture in Britain*. H.M.S.O., London.

26. Clutton-Brock, T. H., Alban, S. D., Gibson, R. M. and Guinness, F. E. (1979) The logical stag: adaptive aspects of fighting in red deer (*Cervus elaphus L.*). *Animal Behaviour* **27**, 211.

27. Codes of Recommendation for the Welfare of Livestock. (a) Code No. 1, *Cattle*; (b) Code No. 3, *Domestic Fowls*. H.M.S.O., London.

28. Coffey, D. J. (1971) The concept of stress. *British Veterinary Journal* **130**, 91.

29. Collias, N. E. and Collias, E. C. (1967) A field study of the Red Junglefowl in North – Central India. *The Condor* **69**, 360.

30. Collias, N. E. and Saichnae, P. (1967) Ecology of the Red Junglefowl in Thailand and Malaya with reference to the origin of domestication. *The Natural History Bulletin of the Siam Society* **22**, 189.

31. Colyer, R. J. (1970) Tail biting in pigs. *Agriculture* **77**, 215.

32. Cooke, F. and McNally, C. M. (1975) Mate selection and colour preferences in lesser snow geese. *Behaviour* **53**, 151.

33. Cooper, R. and Zubeck, J. (1958) Effects of enriched and restricted early environments on the learning ability of bright and dull rats. *Canadian Journal of Psychology* **12**, 159.

34. Darwin, F. (1887) *Life and Letters of Charles Darwin*. John Murray, London. Letter to J. D. Hooker.

35. Darwin, C. (1965) *The Expression of the Emotions in Man and Animals*. The University of Chicago Press.

36. Davis, S. J. M. and Valla, F. R. (1978) Evidence for domestication of the dog 12,000 years ago in the Natufian of Israel. *Nature, London* **276**, 608.

37. Dawkins, M. (1976) Towards an objective method of assessing welfare in domestic fowl. *Applied Animal Ethology* **2**, 245.

38. Dawkins, M. (1977) Do hens suffer in battery cages? Environmental preference and welfare. *Animal Behaviour* **25**, 1034.

39. Delacour, J. (1951) *The Pheasants of the World*. Country Life, London.

40. Donaldson, J. G. S. and Donaldson, F. (1969) *Farming in Britain Today*. Penguin, Harmondsworth.

41. Draper, M. H. and Lake, P. E. (1967) Physiological reactions of the laying fowl to adverse environments, with special reference to the defence reaction. In *Environmental Control in Poultry Production*, edited by T. C. Carter, p. 87. Oliver & Boyd, Edinburgh.

42. Draper, W. A. and Bernstein, I. S. (1963) Stereotyped behavior and cage size. *Perceptual and Motor Skills* **16**, 231.

43. Duncan, I. J. H. (1974) A scientific assessment of welfare. *Proceedings of the British Society for Animal Production* **3**, 9.

44. Duncan, I. J. H. (1977) Behavioural wisdom lost. *Applied Animal Ethology* **3**, 193.

45. Duncan, I. J. H. (1978) The interpretation of preference tests in animal behaviour. *Applied Animal Ethology* **4**, 197.

46. Duncan, I. J. H. and Filshie, J. H. (1979) The use of telemetry devices to measure temperature and heart rate in domestic fowl. In *A Handbook on Biotelemetry and Radio Tracking*, edited by C. J. Amlaner and D. W. Macdonald, p. 579. Pergamon Press, Oxford.

47. Duncan, I. J. H. and Hughes, B. O. (1972) Free and operant feeding in domestic fowls. *Animal Behaviour* **20**, 775.

48. Duncan, I. J. H., Savory, C. J. and Wood-Gush, D. G. M. (1978) Observations on the reproductive behaviour of domestic fowl in the wild. *Applied Animal Ethology* **4**, 29.

49. Durrell, G. (1976) *The Stationary Ark*. Collins, London.

50. Ewbank, R. (1969) Behavioural implications of intensive animal husbandry. *Outlook on Agriculture* **6**, 41.

51. Ewbank, R. (1971) Pigs. In *The UFAW Handbook on the Care and Management of Farm Animals*, p. 140. Churchill Livingstone, Edinburgh.

52. Ewbank, R. (1973) The trouble with being a farm animal. *New Scientist* **60**, 172.

53. Ewbank, R. (1974) Clinical signs of stress in farm animals — changes in behaviour. *British Veterinary Journal* **130**, 90.

54. Ewer, T. K. (1971) Modern animal husbandry systems. In *The UFAW Handbook on the Care and Management of Farm Animals*, p. 1. Churchill Livingstone, Edinburgh.

55. Feekes, F. (1972) 'Irrelevant' ground pecking in agonistic situations in Burmese Red Junglefowl (*Gallus gallus spadiceus*). *Behaviour* **43**, 186.

56. Ferguson, W. (1969) The role of social stress in epidemiology. *British Veterinary Journal* **125**, p. 253.

57. Fouts, R. S. (1973) Aquisition and testing of gestural signs in four young chimpanzees. *Science, New York* **180**, 978.

58. Fox, M. W. ed. (1968) *Abnormal Behavior in Animals*. Saunders, Philadelphia.

59a. Frankham, R. and Weiss, G. M. (1969) Changes in relative aggressiveness of lines selected for part-record egg production under floor housing. *Poultry Science* **48**, 1691.

59b. Frankham, R. and Doornenbal, H. (1970) Physiological differences associated with genetic differences in egg production. I. Organ and endocrine gland weights. *Poultry Science* **49**, 1610.

60. Fraser, D., Ritchie, J. S. D. and Fraser, A. F. (1975) The term 'stress' in a veterinary context. *British Veterinary Journal* **131**, 653.

61. Fraser, A. F. (1968) Behavior disorders in domestic animals. In *Abnormal Behavior in Animals*, edited by M. W. Fox, p. 179. Saunders, Philadelphia.

62. Freedman, D. G., King, J. A. and Elliott, O. (1961) Critical period in the social development of dogs. *Science, New York* **133**, 1016.

63. Gallup, G. G. (1968) Mirror-image stimulation. *Psychological Bulletin* **70**, 782.

64. Gallup, G. G. (1977) Self-recognition in primates. A comparative approach to the bidirectional properties of consciousness. *American Psychologist* **32**, 329.

65. Galston, A. W. and Slayman, C. L. (1979) The not-so-secret life of plants. *American Scientist* **67**, 337.

66. Gardner, B. T. and Gardner, R. A. (1969) Teaching sign language to a chimpanzee. *Science, New York* **165**, 664.

67. Gill, F. B. and Wolf, L. L. (1975) Economics of feeding territoriality in the golden-winged sunbird. *Ecology* **56**, 333.

68. Glover, J. (1977) *Causing Death and Saving Lives*. Penguin, Harmondsworth.

69. Godlovitch, R. (1971) Animals and morals. In *Animals, Men and Morals*, edited by S. Godlovitch, R. Godlovitch and J. Harris, p. 156. Victor Gollancz, London.

70. Griffin, D. R. (1976) *The Question of Animal Awareness*. The Rockefeller University Press, New York.

71. Griffin, D. R. (1978) Prospects for a cognitive ethology. *The Behavioral and Brain Sciences* **1**, 527.

72. Hails, M. R. (1978) Transport stress in animals: a review. *Animal Regulation Studies* **1**, 289.

73. Hanson, R. P. and Karstad, L. (1969) Feral swine in the southeastern United States. *Journal of Wildlife Management* **23**, 64.

74. Hanson, R. S. (1970) Hysteria of mature hens in cages. *Poultry Science* **49**, 1392.

75. Harris, J. (1979) Killing for food. In *Animals' Rights – a Symposium*, edited by D. Paterson and R. D. Ryder, p. 117. Centaur Press, Fontwell, Sussex.

76. Harrison, R. (1970) Steps towards legislation in Great Britain. In *Factory Farming*, edited by J. R. Bellerby, p. 3. B.A.A.S. Education Services, London.

77. Hediger, H. (1955) *Studies of the Psychology and Behaviour of Captive Animals in Zoos and Circuses*. Translated by G. Sircom. Butterworths, London.

78. Hediger, H. (1964) *Wild Animals in Captivity. An Outline of the Biology of Zoological Gardens*. Translated by G. Sircom. Dover Publications, New York.

79. Heiligenberg, W. and Kramer, U. (1972) Aggressiveness as a function of external stimulation. *Journal of Comparative Physiology* **77**, 332.

80. Herrnstein, R. J. and Loveland, D. H. (1964) Complex visual concept in the pigeon. *Science, New York* **146**, 549.

81. Herrnstein, R. J., Loveland, D. H. and Cable, C. (1976) Natural concepts in pigeons. *Journal of Experimental Psychology: Animal Behavior Processes* **2**, 285.

82. Hildén, O. (1965) Habitat selection in birds. *Annales zoologici Societatis zoologico-botanicae fennicae* **2**, 53.

83. Hinde, R. A. (1970) *Animal Behaviour. A Synthesis of Ethology and Comparative Psychology*. McGraw-Hill, New York.

84. Hodos, W. and Campbell, C. B. G. (1969) Scala naturae: why there is no theory in comparative psychology. *Psychological Review* **76**, 337.

85. Holst, D. von (1977) Social stress in Tree-shrews: problems, results and goals. *Journal of Comparative Physiology* **120**, 71.

86. Home Office (1977) *Experiments on Living Animals: Statistics*. Cmnd 7333. H.M.S.O., London.

87. Home Office (1978) *Statistics of Experiments on Living Animals. Great Britain*. Cmnd 7628. H.M.S.O., London.

88. Houston, A. I. and McFarland, D. J. (1980) Behavioral resilience and its relation to demand functions. In *Limits to Action: the Allocation of Individual Behavior*, edited by J. E. R. Staddon, p. 177. Academic Press, New York.

89. Howard, B. R. (1974) The assessment of stress in poultry. *British Veterinary Journal* **130**, 88.

90. Hubbard, J. I. (1975) *The Biological Bases of Mental Activity*. Addison-Wesley, Reading, Mass.

91. Hughes, B. O. (1976) Preference decisions of domestic hens for wire or litter floors. *Applied Animal Ethology* **2**, 155.

92. Hughes, B. O. (1978) Behavioural needs. *The Veterinary Record* **103**, 165.

93. Hughes, B. O. and Black, A. J. (1973) The preference of domestic hens for different types of battery cage floor. *British Poultry Science* **14**, 615.

94. Hume, C. W. (1967) The legal protection of laboratory animals. In *The UFAW Handbook on the Care and Management of Laboratory Animals*, 3rd edn. Edited by UFAW. E. & S. Livingstone, London.

95. Humphrey, N. K. (1972) 'Interest' and 'pleasure': two determinants of a monkey's visual preferences. *Perception* **1**, 395.

96. Humphrey, N. K. (1978) Nature's psychologists. *New Scientist* **78**, 900.

97. Hutt, F. B. (1949) *Genetics of the Fowl*. McGraw-Hill, New York.

98. Hyams, E. (1972) *Animals in the Service of Man*. Dent, London.

99. Iersel, J. J. A. van and Bol, A. C. A. (1958) Preening of two tern species. A study on displacement activities. *Behaviour* **13**, 1.

100. Immelmann, K. (1972) Sexual and other long-term aspects of imprinting in birds and other species. In *Advances in the Study of Behavior*, Vol. 4, edited by D. S. Lehrman, R. A. Hinde and E. Shaw, p. 147. Academic Press, New York.

101. James, F. W. and Foenander, F. (1961) Social behaviour studies on domestic animals. *Australian Journal of Agricultural Research* **12**, 1239.

102. Jansen, P. E., Goodman, E. D., Jowaisas, D. and Bunnell, B. N. (1969) Paper as a positive reinforcer for acquisition of a bar press response by the golden hamster. *Psychonomic Science* **16**, 113.

103. Jewell, P. A., Milner, C. and Morton Boyd, J. (eds.) (1974) *Island Survivors: the Ecology of the Soay Sheep of St. Kilda*. Athlone Press, University of London.

104. Johnson, R. A. (1963) Habitat preference and behavior of breeding Jungle Fowl in Central Western Thailand. *Wilson Bulletin* **75**, 270.

105. Jürgens, U. (1979) Vocalization as an emotional indicator. A neuroethological study in the squirrel monkey. *Behaviour* **69**, 88.

106. Keele, C. A. and Smith, R. (eds.) (1962) *The Assessment of Pain in Man and Animals*. UFAW, published by E. & S. Livingstone, London.

107. Keiper, R. R. (1969) Causal factors of stereotypies in caged birds. *Animal Behaviour* **17**, 114.

108. Kerr, F. W. L. and Casey, K. L. (1978) Pain. *Neurosciences Research Program Bulletin* **16** (1).

109. Kettlewell, H. B. D. (1955) Selection experiments on industrial melanism in the Lepidoptera. *Heredity* **9**, 323.

110. Kettlewell, H. B. D. and Conn, D. L. T. (1977) Further background – choice experiments on cryptic Lepidoptera. *Journal of Zoology* **181**, 371.

111. Kiley-Worthington, M. (1977) *Behavioural Problems of Farm Animals*. Oriel Press, Stocksfield.

112. Kilgour, R. (1976) The contributions of psychology to a knowledge of farm animal behaviour. *Applied Animal Ethology* **2**, 197.

113. Kilgour, R. and de Langen, H. (1970) Stress in sheep resulting from management practices. *Proceedings of the New Zealand Society of Animal Production* **30**, 65.

114. Klopfer, P. H. and Hailman, J. P. (1965) Habitat selection in birds. In *Advances in the Study of Behavior*, Vol. 1, edited by D. S. Lehrman, R. A. Hinde and E. Shaw, p. 279. Academic Press, New York.

115. Klopfer, P. H. and Hailman, J. P. (1967) *An Introduction to Animal Behavior: Ethology's First Century*. Prentice-Hall, New Jersey.

116. Koehler, O. (1951) The ability of birds to 'count'. *Bulletin of Animal Behaviour* **9**, 41.

117. Köhler, W. (1925) *The Mentality of Apes*. Translated by E. Winter. Routledge & Kegan Paul, London.

118. Kortlandt, A. (1940) Eine Übersicht der angeborenen Verhaltungsweisen des Mittel-Europäischen Kormorans (*Phalacrocorax carbo sinensis*). *Archives néerlandaises de Zoologie* **14**, 401.

119. Kruijt, J. P. (1964) Ontogeny of social behaviour in Burmese red junglefowl (*Gallus gallus spadiceus Bonnaterra*). *Behaviour*, Supplement 12.

120. Kruuk, H. (1972) Surplus killing by carnivores. *Journal of Zoology* **166**, 233.

121. Kruuk, H. (1972) *The Spotted Hyena*. University of Chicago Press, Chicago.

122. Kruuk, H. (1976) The biological function of gulls' attraction towards predators. *Animal Behaviour* **24**, 146.

123. Kurz, J. C. and Marchinton, R. L. (1972) Radiotelemetry studies of feral hogs in S. Carolina. *Journal of Wildlife Management* **36**, 1240.

124. Lack, D. (1937) The psychological factor in bird distribution. *British Birds* **31**, 130.

125. Lack, D. (1954) *The Natural Regulation of Animal Numbers*. Oxford University Press.

126. Lagerspetz, K. M. J. (1969) Aggression and aggressiveness in laboratory mice. In *Aggressive Behavior*, edited by S. Garattini and E. B. Sigg, p. 77, Excerpta Medica, Amsterdam.

127. Levine, S. (1971) Stress and behavior. *Scientific American* **224**, 26.

128. Littlewood, S. (1965) Chairman. Report of the Departmental Committee on Experiments on Animals. Cmnd 2641. H.M.S.O., London.

129. Lorenz, K. Z. (1952) *King Solomon's Ring*. Methuen, London.

130. Losey, G. S. and Margules, L. (1974) Cleaning symbiosis provides a positive reinforcer for fish. *Science, New York* **184**, 179.

131. Lowry, D. C. and Abplanalp, H. (1972) Social dominance difference, given limited access to common food, between hens selected and unselected for increased egg production. *British Poultry Science* **13**, 365.

132. Lubow, R. E. (1974) High-order concept formation in the pigeon. *Journal of the Experimental Analysis of Behavior* **21**, 475.

133. McBride, G. (1970) The social control of behaviour in fowls. In *Aspects of Poultry Behaviour*, edited by B. M. Freeman and R. F. Gordon, p. 3. British Poultry Science, Edinburgh.

134. McBride, G., Parer, I. P. and Foenander, F. (1969) The social organization and behaviour of the feral domestic fowl. *Animal Behaviour Monographs* **2**, 127.

135. Macdonald, D. W. and Dawkins, M. (1980) Ethology – the science and the tool. In *Animal Experimentation*, edited by D. Sperlinger, in press. John Wiley, Chichester.

136. Marsh, J. T., Lavender, J. F., Chang, S.-S. and Rasmussen, A. F. (1963) Poliomyelitis in monkeys: decreased susceptibility after avoidance stress. *Science, New York* **140**, 1414.

137. Mason, J. W. (1975) Emotion as reflected in patterns of endocrine integration. In *Emotions – their Parameters and*

Measurement, edited by L. Levi, p. 143. Raven Press, New York.

138. Masserman, J. H. (1950) Experimental neuroses. *Scientific American* **182**, 38.

139. Medawar, P. (1972) *The Hope of Progress*. Methuen, London.

140. Melzack, R. (1973) *The Puzzle of Pain*. Penguin, Harmondsworth.

141. Melzack, R. and Wall, P. D. (1965) Pain mechanisms: a new theory. *Science, New York* **150**, 971.

142. Menzel, E. W. (1972) Spontaneous invention of ladders in a group of young chimpanzees. *Folia Primatologica* **17**, 87.

143. Menzel, E. W. (1973) Further observations on the use of ladders in a group of young chimpanzees. *Folia Primatologica* **19**, 450.

144. Mersky, H. and Spear, F. G. (1967) *Pain: Psychological and Psychiatric Aspects*. Baillière, Tindall and Cassell, London.

145. Meyer-Holzapfel, M. (1968) Abnormal behavior in zoo animals. In *Abnormal Behavior in Animals*, edited by M. W. Fox, p. 476. Saunders, Philadelphia.

146. Midgley, M. M. (1970) *Intensive Poultry Management for Egg Production*. MAFF Bulletin No. 152. H.M.S.O., London.

147. Morgan, M. J. and Nicholas, D. J. (1979) Discrimination between reinforced action patterns in the rat. *Learning and Motivation* **10**, 1.

148. Morris, D. (1964) The response of animals to a restricted environment. *Symposium of the Zoological Society of London* **13**, 99.

149. Mouin, G. (1976) Language, communication, chimpanzees. *Current Anthropology* **17**, 1.

150. Mountcastle, V. B (1974) Pain and temperature sensibilities. In *Medical Physiology*, Vol. I, edited by V. B. Mountcastle, p. 348. Mosby, St Louis.

151. Murphy, L. B. (1978) A review of animal welfare and intensive animal production. *Report of Queensland Department of Primary Industries*.

152. Nagel, T. (1974) What is it like to be a bat? *Philosophical Review* **83**, 435.

153. Orians, G. (1971) Ecological aspects of behavior. In *Avian Biology*, Vol. I, edited by D. S. Farner and J. R. King, p. 513. Academic Press, London and New York.

154. Parsons, P. A. (1967) *the Genetic Analysis of Behaviour*.

Methuen, London.

155. Partridge, L. (1978) Habitat selection. In *Behavioural Ecology. An Evolutionary Approach*, edited by J. R. Krebs and N. B. Davies, p. 351. Blackwell Scientific Publications, Oxford.

156. Patterson, F. G. (1978) The gestures of a gorilla: sign language acquisition in another pongid. *Brain and Language* 5, 72.

157. Perry, G. C. (1978) Behavioural needs. *The Veterinary Record* 102, 386.

158. Pfaffenberger, C. J., Scott, J. P., Fuller, J. L., Ginsburg, B. E. and Bielfelt, S. W. (1976) *Guide Dogs for the Blind: their Selection, Development and Training*. Developments in Animal and Veterinary Sciences, 1. Elsevier, Amsterdam.

159. Premack, D. (1972) Teaching language to an ape. *Scientific American* 227, 92.

160. Protsch, R. and Berger, R. (1973) Earliest radiocarbon dates for domesticated animals. *Science, New York* 179, 235.

161. Putten, van G. and Dammers, J. (1976) A comparative study of the well-being of piglets reared conventionally and in cages. *Applied Animal Ethology* 2, 339.

162. Ray, P. M. and Scott, W. N. (1973) Animal welfare legislation in the E.E.C. *British Veterinary Journal* 129, 194.

163. Reed, C. A. (1959) Animal domestication in the prehistoric Near East. *Science, New York* 130, 1629.

164. Romanes, G. J. (1883) *Mental Evolution in Animals*. Kegan Paul Trench, London.

165. Roper, T. J. (1976) Self-sustaining activities and reinforcement in the nest building behaviour of mice. *Behaviour* 59, 40.

166. Ruckebusch, Y. (1975) The hypnogram as an index of adaptation of farm animals to changes in their environment. *Applied Animal Ethology* 2, 3.

167. Russell, B. (1930) *The Conquest of Happiness*. Unwin, London.

168. Russell, W. M. S. and Burch, R. L. (1959) *The Principles of Humane Experimental Technique*. Methuen, London.

169. Ryder, R. D. (1975) *Victims of Science*. Davis-Poynter, London. (Especially pp. 32 and 37.)

170. Sackett, G. P. and Ruppenthal, G. C. (1973) Development of monkeys after varied experiences during infancy. In *Ethology and Development*, edited by S. A. Barnett, p. 52. Heinemann, London.

171. Sainsbury, D. W. B. (1971) Domestic fowls. In *The UFAW Handbook on the Care and Management of Farm Animals*, p. 99. Churchill Livingstone, Edinburgh.

172. Savage-Rumbaugh, E. S., Rumbaugh, D. M. and Boysen, S. (1978) Linguistically-mediated tool use and exchange by chimpanzees (*Pan troglodytes*) *The Behavioral and Brain Sciences* 1, 539.

173. Schachter, S. (1970) The assumption of identity and peripheralist-centralist controversies in motivation and emotion. In *Feelings and Emotion*, edited by M. Arnold, p. 111. Academic Press, New York.

174. Schachter, S. and Singer, J. E. (1962) Cognitive, social, and physiological determinants of emotional state. *Psychological Review* 69, 379.

175. Schutz, F. (1965) Sexuelle Prägung bei Anatiden. *Zeitschrift für Tierpsychologie* 22, 50.

176. Selye, H. (1952) *The Story of the Adaptation Syndrome*. Acta, Montreal.

177. Selye, H. (1974) *Stress without Distress*. Hodder and Stoughton, London.

178. Shallice, T. (1978) The dominant action system: an information-processing approach to consciousness. In *The Stream of Consciousness: Scientific Investigations into the Flow of Human Experience*, edited by K. S. Pope and J. L. Singer, p. 117. Plenum Press, New York.

179. Sheehan, P. W. (1978) Mental imagery. In *Psychology Survey*, No. 1, edited by B. M. Foss, p. 58. George Allen & Unwin, London.

180. Shepard, R. N. (1978) The mental image. *The American Psychologist* 33, 125.

181. Shuster, S. (1977) Why we need animal research. *World Medicine* 13 (5), 19.

182. Siegel, R. K. and Honig, W. K. (1970) Pigeon concept formation: successive and simultaneous acquisition. *Journal of the Experimental Analysis of Behavior* 13, 385.

183. Siegel, P. B. (1975) Behavioural Genetics. In *The Behaviour of Domestic Animals*, 3rd edn., edited by E. S. E. Hafez, p. 20. Baillière Tindall, London.

184. Signoret, J. P., Baldwin, B. A., Fraser, D. and Hafez, E. S. E. (1975) The behaviour of swine. In *The Behaviour of Domestic Animals*, 3rd edn., edited by E. S. E. Hafez, p. 295. Baillière

Tindall, London.

185. Singer, P. (1976) *Animal Liberation*. Jonathan Cape, London.

186. Skinner, B. F. (1963) Behaviorism at fifty. *Science, New York* **140**, 951.

187. Sluckin, W. (1972) *Imprinting and Early Learning*, 2nd edn. Methuen, London.

188. Smyth, D. H. (1978) *Alternatives to Animal Experiments*. Scolar Press, London.

189. Spencer, H. (1880) *Principles of Psychology*, 3rd edn. Longmans, London.

190. Spurway, H. (1953) Can wild animals be kept in captivity? *New Biology* **13**, 11.

191. Stettner, L. J. and Matyniak, K. A. (1968) The brain of birds. *Scientific American* **218**, 64.

192. Stevenson, J. (1967) Reinforcing effects of chaffinch song. *Animal Behaviour* **15**, 427.

193. Thompson, R., Melzack, R. and Scott, T. H. (1956) 'Whirling behavior' in dogs as related to early experience. *Science, New York* **123**, 939.

194. Thompson, T. I. (1963) Visual reinforcement in Siamese fighting fish. *Science, New York* **141**, 55.

195. Thorpe, W. H. (1965) The assessment of pain and distress in animals. In *Report of the Technical Committee to Enquire into the Welfare of Animals kept under Intensive Livestock Systems*. Chairman: F. W. R. Brambell. Cmnd 2836. H.M.S.O., London.

196. Thorpe, W. H. (1967) Discussion to Part II of *Environmental Control in Poultry Production*, edited by T. C. Carter, p. 125. Oliver & Boyd, Edinburgh.

197. Thorpe, W. H. (1969) Welfare of domestic animals. *Nature, London* **224**, 18.

198. Tinbergen, N. (1951) *The Study of Instinct*. Clarendon Press, Oxford.

199. Tinbergen, N. (1952) 'Derived activities': their causation, biological significance, origin and emancipation during evolution. *Quarterly Review of Biology* **27**, 1.

200. Toates, F. M. and Archer, J. A. (1978) A comparative review of motivational systems using classical control theory. *Animal Behaviour* **26**, 368.

201. Tompkins, P. and Bird, C. (1973) *The Secret Life of Plants*. Harper & Row, New York and London.

202. Trivers, R. L. (1971) The evolution of reciprocal altruism. *Quarterly Review of Biology* **46**, 35.

203. Tudge, C. (1973) Farmers in loco parentis. *New Scientist* **60**, 179.

204. Universities Federation for Animal Welfare. Report 1977 – 78. UFAW, Potters Bar.

205. Watson, J. B. (1924) *Psychology from the Standpoint of a Behaviorist*, 2nd edn. Lippincott, Philadelphia.

206. Wells, M. J. (1978) *Octopus. Physiology and Behaviour of an Advanced Invertebrate*. Chapman and Hall, London.

207. Wilson, H. C. (1971) Beef cattle and veal calves. In *The UFAW Handbook on the Care and Management of Farm Animals*, p. 39. Churchill Livingstone, Edinburgh.

208. Wood-Gush, D. G. M. (1959) A history of the domestic chicken from antiquity to the 19th century. *Poultry Science* **38**, 321.

209. Wood-Gush, D. G. M. (1972) Strain differences in response to sub-optimal stimuli in the fowl. *Animal Behaviour* **20**, 72.

210. Wood-Gush, D. G. M., Duncan, I. J. H. and Fraser, D. (1975) Social stress and welfare problems in agricultural animals. In *The Behaviour of Domestic Animals*, edited by E. S. E. Hafez, p. 182. Baillière Tindall, London.

211. Wood-Gush, D. G. M. and Duncan, I. J. H. (1976) Some behavioural observations on domestic fowl in the wild. *Applied Animal Ethology* **2**, 255.

212. Zeuner, F. E. (1954) Domestication of animals. In *A History of Technology*, Vol. I, edited by C. Singer, E. J. Holmyard and A. R. Hall, p. 327. Clarendon Press, Oxford.

Index